Lollipo

Lollipops & Rainbows

Teaching Literacy with Soul

By Clare Ford
&
The "Switched On" Children & Teens
from Around the World

Lollipops and Rainbows

PUBLISHER

Copyright © 2020 Clare Ford

All rights reserved.

The author asserts the moral right under the
Copyright, Designs and Patents Act 1988 to be
identified as the author of this work.

All Rights reserved. No part of this publication may
be reproduced, stored in a retrieval system or
transmitted, in any form or by any means without
the prior consent of the author, nor be otherwise
circulated in any form of binding or cover other
than that which it is published and without a similar
condition being imposed on the subsequent
purchaser.

Lollipops and Rainbows

DEDICATION

This book and learning resource is dedicated to
all the children who will lead us into the light.

ACKNOWLEDGMENTS

I would like to say a massive "thank you" to EVERYONE who has collaborated in this book – you will find incredible writing and fabulous illustrations that have been submitted by the following children and young adults:

Dóireann Cahill
Tomás Cahill
Emilia Catanach
Lucy Chandler
Ellie Clements
Daniil Domnych
Emily Dowsett
Lucy Dowsett
Nelly E'beyer
Alex Ford
Oskar Ford
Scarlett Hodder
Malak Mahmood
Yousif Mahmood
Fedora Mensah
Devlin O'Brien
Ted Parkinson-Hill
Lillian Strickland
Mia Waterworth

And of course thank you to the parents and adult family members who have supported their children with this project during extremely challenging times.

I would also like to thank my lovely partner John for his unwavering support, my mother Jill for her editing skills and the publishing team at Dreaming Big Together publishing for believing in this project.

Together, we are stronger. Thank you all.

HOW TO USE THIS BOOK

For parents and educators:

This book is for YOU!

Here are some suggested ways for you to get the most out of it:

1) You can work your way through it, using the teaching resources at the back to help you teach your child to write in different genres and styles with key techniques and features.

2) You can simply choose a story to read to or with your child for enjoyment, and follow up with the "Aligned Activities" and the "Magical Meditation" if you would like to.

3) For more reluctant readers and writers, you could start with the Magical Meditation before a suggested follow-up activity, using children's writing as an example of what can be achieved.

The KEY to unlocking the creative potential inside your student is to ask them if they are enjoying the story, activity or meditation, and open up a discussion using the prompts under "Curious Questions".

Enjoy teaching literacy with soul!

Clare x

Clare Ford
Founder of **SwitchedON**!

Artemis' Birthday, *by Clare Ford* — 7

Suggested Follow-Up Activities — 11

Magical Meditation — 12

When Spirit Wolf Lost Her Spirit, *by Clare Ford* — 14

Suggested Follow-Up Activities — 18

Magical Meditation — 19

The Great Escape of Mulberry Farm, *by Lucy Chandler* — 20

How the Earth Was Made, *by Clare Ford* — 30

Suggested Follow-Up Activities — 32

Magical Meditation — 33

Magic Behind the Waterfall, *by Emily Dowsett* — 34

Atlantica, by Nelly E'beyer — 38

A Recipe for Sunshine, *by Clare Ford* — 54

Suggested Follow-Up Activities — 56

Magical Meditation — 57

A Letter to My Heart, *by Clare Ford* — 60

Suggested Follow-Up Activities — 62

Magical Meditation — 63

The Planet of Mortals and Mystics, *by Ellie Clements* — 64

Swan's Song, *by Clare Ford* — 68

Suggested Follow-Up Activities — 70

Magical Meditation — 72

Detective Darcy & the Missing Donuts, *by Emilia Catanach* — 74

A Song for Humanity, *by Clare Ford* — 79

Lollipops and Rainbows

Suggested Follow-Up Activities	80
Magical Meditation	81
What Lurks Within the Temple? *by Tomás Cahill*	83
Who Am I? by Clare Ford	85
Suggested Follow-Up Activities	89
Magical Meditation	90
Threat to Teddy Mountain, *by Scarlett Hodder*	91
Daisy's Diary, by Fedora Mensah	96
A Prayer to the Universe, *by Clare Ford*	100
Suggested Follow-Up Activities	101
Magical Meditation	102
An Adventure into the Amazon. *by Chloe Dowsett*	103
Diary Entry: The Journey, *by Clare Ford*	107
Suggested Follow-Up Activities	109
Magical Meditation	**112**
The World of Pandora, *by Yousif Mahmood*	**113**
The Magic Big Mac, *by Daniil Domnych*	**118**
Guided Rainbow Meditation	**121**
The Return of Fruit Island, *by Malak Mahmood*	**123**
Grassy Meadows *by Mia Waterworth*	**127**
Meet The Authors & Illustrators	**132**
Teaching Notes compiled by Clare Ford	**138**

As my Granny always used to say…

"ARE YOU SITTING COMFORTABLY?
THEN LET US BEGIN…"

GENRE: FICTION: CREATIVE WRITING – MYTH/LEGEND

Artemis' Birthday

Written by Clare Ford,
Illustrated by Alex Ford

Artemis was no ordinary girl, and so her birthday was going to be like no other.

Long, long, ago deep in the forgotten mists of time, the faint hooting of an owl was carried on a soft breeze to an ancient woodland grove, where Artemis was resting in her favourite place, against the gnarled fallen log of a great oak tree. Artemis was waiting for her father, who was meeting her to give her a present for her tenth birthday.

Needless to say, she could barely contain her excitement and waiting seemed like an eternity. "Practise patience my dear," she could almost hear her grandmother whispering to her. So, with a deep breath, she sat up straight, with her feet firmly planted on the ground, and raised her face to the sunlight that was streaming through the treetops.

Within seconds, Artemis could feel her breathing slowing,

and calm light wash through her.

She caught her reflection in the sparkling stream flowing next to her, and thought how her golden hair looked like sunbeams.

Now that Artemis had quietened her mind and body, the forest animals began to shyly approach her with their birthday gifts.

Artemis started humming and singing, softly at first and then chanting nature's song. Soon, the woodland sparrows and hawks were joining the deer, fox, owl, rabbit and badger that had come to see Artemis.

Suddenly, she heard the rustle of leaves, and drumming of hooves. Then silence. She felt something behind her. She stopped breathing.

Silhouetted in the flickering light was a giant shadow – of a bear, but not the brown bear she was used to seeing in these woods.

Her father was taking too long. The shadows spread and lengthened through the trees, throwing dappled patterns onto the forest floor. Anxiously, she estimated the time again.

Could it be him?

Coming closer.

Something felt strange...

As time went on, other creatures appeared too, such as the wolf, eagle and bear. Artemis was unafraid and sat quietly and still so that she could fully appreciate the gifts that each animal brought her.

Eventually, as the sun was setting low and the wood was awash with a golden glow, Zeus appeared.

"You have done well my daughter," he re-assured her. "And now it is time for your special gift!"

Artemis sat close to her father, sheltered from the breeze by his huge body and warm cloak, wrapped protectively in his strong arm. She looked into his strong, kind face and saw the deep wisdom in his clear eyes.

She knew instinctively that this would be a gift like no other – for her father was Zeus, God of the Gods.

Carefully unwrapping the moss and leaves from the bundle that her father had given her, Artemis discovered she was holding a wooden box. A wooden box that was similar to the one at home that her grandmother kept her special rings in. A wooden box that felt ancient and very, very special. Artemis carefully traced the engravings etched on the curved lid with her index finger, trying to fathom the symbols that she found there.

"What is in this box papa?" she thought breathlessly...

"This is the box of the ancients," he explained, "It has been handed down to specially chosen people, who are the guardians and light workers of the Earth. And now, my daughter Artemis, I am handing this box to you. In it are the answers to all questions – asked and as yet unasked. In it is the wisdom of the ancients from the beginning of Dawn."

"But why should I have this box?" asked Artemis nervously.

"Because you have been chosen. And because one day you will have a deep and powerful knowledge to add to the box, which will continue to help children when they need guidance."

With a beating heart and trembling hands, she carefully began to open the box...

Illustrated by Alex Ford

SUGGESTED FOLLOW-UP ACTIVITIES

Curious Questions:

1. How would you feel if you received a present like this for your birthday? Why?
2. What spiritual question would you like answered?

Aligned Actions:

1. Sketch, draw or paint the woodland setting that Artemis was waiting in
2. Name each animal that came to see Artemis. What present do you think they brought her? Think about the attributes of each animal – for example, a fox is cunning.
3. Listen to some music for this story and make up your own movements or mimes
4. Compile your very own "Dragon Guide" – how could you tame a dragon that stole your special gift?
5. Write out a simple character description as a mind map for your favourite character in the story.

Magic Meditation:

Imagine sitting on a gnarly log in the middle of a beautiful wood with a stream nearby.

What can you see, hear, smell and feel?

Take some deep breaths in and out and feel your heart rate and breathing slow down.

Can you feel the warm sun? The cool breeze?

Can you hear the gurgling stream? The birds singing?

Can you feel the bark of the oak tree? The moss under your feet?

Take some more deep breaths.

Notice your heart beating slower.

Notice your breathing.

Smile to yourself as you enjoy this special moment.

Then, very slowly, wiggle your fingers and toes and come back to the room.

Rainbow Wolf, Illustrated by Ted Parkinson-Hill

Lollipops and Rainbows

GENRE: FICTION: CREATIVE WRITING –
MYTHS & LEGENDS

When Spirit Wolf Lost Her Spirit

Written by Clare Ford,
Illustrated by Alex Ford & Ted Parkisnon-Hill

Never in history had such an event occurred. In the centre of a leafy glade, Spirit Wolf was lying, still and exhausted.

Moon Wolf howled, long and low, to summon Mother Nature to help. The wind rustled the leaves in the glade, and woodland creatures crept out to surround Spirit Wolf. "What shall we do?" they wondered...

"Is Spirit Wolf ill? What has happened? Has Spirit Wolf lost her spirit?" Fire Wolf stood up amongst the pack and suggested that they make a medicine wheel from twigs and leaves. This wheel points to the four corners of the earth and to the heavens above and the earth below.

Since the dawn of time it has been used to summon wisdom from the ancients to heal earthly suffering.

Guardian Wolf took charge, as she had been handed ancient knowledge and wisdom in the form of visions and asked for guidance to heal Spirit Wolf.

"We need to get Spirit Wolf to the Worry Tree," she explained gravely. "Something is troubling her heart and soul and the Worry Tree will listen and take the worries away. Then Spirit Wolf can heal and will feel strengthened." So, with that, the pack of wolves and the woodland creatures made a bed of straw and moss which they used to carry Spirit Wolf carefully over the rocky terrain to the lonely Worry Tree on the edge of the plain. They laid her down with care.

They stood in a respective circle around her and sent beautiful pink sparkling healing energy from their hearts to each other, to Spirit Wolf and to all of the Earth.

Quietly, Howling Wolf started a slow humming, and the other wolves gently joined in until the wheel of medicine lifted itself up from the barren soil and span above Spirit Wolf's body, this way and that, swirling and whirling until all that could be seen was a myriad of colours.

A bright translucent rainbow surrounded Spirit Wolf's body and a beautiful white glow lit up the area under the Worry Tree.

The pack of wolves and woodland creatures increased their humming and chanting so that the Eagles on far away mountains and Salmon in deep, cool streams could hear them too.

Slowly, Spirit Wolf began to stir, and then, wobbly and unbalanced at first, to stand.

Then she stretched, looked up to the sky above and emitted a long, beautiful eerie howl which reverberated around the earth, to all dimensions, to all galaxies and stars in the Universe.

"My journey has brought me home. I have found what I was searching for. It is within me.

I have everything I need inside of me, in my heart and in my soul. I thought my spirit was shattered into hundreds of little tiny pieces, but now I feel whole again. Thank you."

The wolves and creatures cheered and went back to the glade, rejoicing that Spirit Wolf felt whole again.

Lollipops and Rainbows

Illustrated by Alex Ford

SUGGESTED FOLLOW-UP ACTIVITIES

Curious Questions:

1. Discuss the moral of the story. How does this make you feel? What does it mean?
2. What do you feel like when you feel "whole"? How is this different to feeling "broken" or "shattered"?

Aligned Actions:

1. Write your worries or concerns on a leaf template and then hang them on a Worry Tree. Then choose a leaf and quietly use your inner voice to tell you the solution to the problem... write the solution on the back of the leaf and put it back on the Worry Tree
2. Stand in a circle and quietly start humming the first note that comes to mind... wait until other people join in so that you make a circle of sound. Stop when you feel guided to do so.
3. Re-write this legend as a play script and act it out in groups, using your own sound effects and stage directions. Discuss how each group has interpreted the story differently.
4. Write a diary entry or adventure about a She-wolf.

Magic Meditation:

Imagine sitting under a worry tree with a heavy heart...

Take some deep breaths and with each breath send your worries to the tree.

Begin to feel lighter as your burdens are lifted.

Now with each breath feel the earth under you, the gnarled tree trunk against your back and the sun on your face.

Feel the light around you getting softer and lighter as you become surrounded by a rainbow...

Imagine you can feel the rainbow light entering every cell of your body, every fibre of your being, every gap between every cell.

You are a Rainbow Child.

Breathe in this truth and feel your heart and soul fill up and overflow with rainbow light.

Then, very slowly, wiggle your fingers and toes and come back to the room.

The Great Escape Of Mulberry Farm

Written and Illustrated by Lucy Chandler

Chapter 1

Mulberry Farm, where I used to live was a raggedy, squashed barn beside a decrepit, eerie looking barn house.

A huge birch sign with the words MULBERRY FARM emblazoned in the middle stood at the entrance. The barn had a crimson roof with holes in the top and a birch plank floor riddled with rats and covered in low quality, scratchy, marigold yellow straw; it was made 83 years ago in 1805.

This is the diary of an adorable, taffy animal with bright, ebony eyes and peppercorn black lashes (I'm a piglet if you haven't realised).

Lollipops and Rainbows

And before you think I am completely insane and try and arrange therapy for me because you can't write with hoofs, I'm writing this with my tail not my hoofs because you're right, I can't write with hoofs.

To answer your other questions, I'm writing this with a dead wood pigeon's feather, this is ink make from stinging nettles, my name is Josie and, since I am mean, I won't tell you where I live - to find that out you will have to read on.

I have two friends I'm here with at the moment – Summer, an intelligent sheep with a porcelain, white fluffy clouds of wool surrounding a pearly white animal who stares into space with butterscotch eyes and an obsidian, horizontal line for a pupil. May is the energetic, tawny Jersey calf with pearly white legs. May is beautiful and takes after her mother, Bessie with majestic, long lashes framing midnight black eyes with a button nose in front.

Chapter 2

It all started on 13th June 1888 when we overheard Mr. Davis instructing the farm hand, "Remember, get the pig nice and fat for Christmas or we'll have a terrible Christmas dinner. Make sure you feed the skinny thing every day."

Suddenly I imagined being served as bacon and sausages at Christmas, the most wonderful time of the year. May and Summer are really lucky because they have wool and milk to give instead of themselves. Ever since then Summer, May and I have been planning to escape from the barn to see the world and its many beautiful habitats (well not the world, just Yorkshire but I'm trying to make it more exciting.)

And tonight, was that night.

The escape had gone well, in the dead of night, hours after evening fell and the sky turned marigold, apricot and fuchsia – we escaped when the sky was onyx black and only the silhouettes of trees were visible basking in the moon's dimmed, lace white glow.

We were just about to disappear forever into the eerie woods, when a small, macaroon yellow light appeared. We froze. Had we been well and truly BUSTED before our exciting adventure had even begun?

Luckily, the candle was blown out creating a silver gas that spread itself out into the small cramped room. We started to trot out and when we were finally miles deep in a pine wood I dared to ask, "Guys are we missing something in our plan?"

Summer replied, "Nope" seconds before May added playfully, "No way José" - at least that made me giggle but then we all got a horrible feeling...

"WHERE ARE WE GOING?!" we screamed in unison, creating an interrobang.

"No chance of getting back now," May muttered lifelessly. We all agreed.

So, on and on we went through an enormous, juniper green wood until dawn finally fell and light flushed throughout the northern countryside of England.

The sky turned into a beautiful, luminescent sunrise and the clouds turned candy floss pink which were easily visible with a background of a vast, honey yellow sky.

We scavenged all morning and afternoon searching for food as each of us learned the world's true wonderment for the first time. Although my usual carrot, apple and potato breakfast is quite nice, I much prefer nuts and berries. We soon entered a flowery field just as dawn was breaking and lay there happily talking and playing.

Young adults regularly passed by enjoying the sunshine whilst feeding us cakes and biscuits (although they were pretty new inventions). May and Summer grazed quietly and calmly but since pigs don't eat grass, I ate from the strawberry plants nearby and when I had finished most of those, I even ate a few of the flowers!

As night fell, we dozed off in a patch of overgrown moss in front of another massive wood planning to set off there in the morning.

As the sun came up, we trekked further into the wood and carried off the remainders of what we had been fed the day before in a discarded top hat, so we could eat it later on in our journey when food was scarce and we were starving. Our trip through these woods was very similar to the one before and we saw a sign saying JUDY WOOD.

We slowly sauntered through Judy Wood but little did we know it would turn into our worst nightmare...

Chapter 3

Not long after we entered Judy Wood, the sun sank behind the trees, turning the sky into a blackened pit of darkness with hundreds of bright candles lighting the way. As soon as the sun disappeared, we were terror-stricken and the once beautiful world we knew turned into a horror story.

There was a harsh neigh in the distance and the thump that followed it was enough to paralyze us with fear.

The horse had died. May ran off screaming.

Summer made a gesture to bite her wool; I bit as hard as I could and we took off.

After what seemed like hours, Summer came to a sudden halt as we saw a cow's corpse on the ground.   It couldn't be…

Yes, it could. It was May. Tears stung my eyes.

When I could finally see again, two huge, glistening, sharp teeth were visible followed by a pair of beady red eyes which were watching my every move. Could all of our lives come to an end?

Chapter 4

As the figure stepped out of the shadows, I realised what it was. It was a wolf.

Once again, I froze with fear. The wolf bared its teeth and opened his mouth wide. Then it all went black.

When my eyes were next open and my senses came back to me, I saw Summer shaking me wildly, obviously trying to wake me up from my faint. I asked her how long I'd been there. "Um, three seconds. I lost May but I'm not going to lose you!" Summer replied.

After Summer told me this, I realised that what had been staring at me was still out there, out there very close. My thoughts were interrupted by a low growling sound and I stared at Summer as she stared at me.

I grabbed onto her thick, woollen coat with my teeth and we fled from May (I just hope she forgives us in the next life). As soon as Summer stopped (actually I did 3 seconds before) we dropped on the floor – dead from exhaustion.

I'm just kidding!!! We were just really tired since we hadn't slept at all that night and the sky was getting lighter. We were cut and aching from running through thorns so rapidly.

When we were both awake, we sat about happily snacking on Victoria sponge and biscuit leftovers when Summer's eyes grew as big as saucers and she froze, trying to speak but all that came out was silence. Eventually, I picked up the courage to look behind me; it was the wolf!

I wanted to run but I was frozen. He bared his teeth. I was going to be dead. I couldn't escape.

Lollipops and Rainbows

I was dead meat (literally). Sharp, pointed teeth were so close to my ear I could smell his minty breath.

"Ouch!" she said, "Those look nasty. I've got this cranberry juice - did you know cranberries have healing powers?"

I gulped - was this just a dog?

"N-n-no, I d-d-didn't," I stammered nervously.

"Here! I'll help! It might sting though." It did sting but after a while, with the help of some rosemary, I was fine along with Summer.

"Hi I'm Adolpha, which means noble, kind she-wolf in German!"

I know she was actually quite friendly and we didn't have to run away from Adolpha, but would you stop to chat to a she-wolf in the middle of a spooky forest?

I asked her what had killed May, and Adolpha said she watched May galloping off like she had mad cow disease and May harmlessly ran into a tree and blacked-out, but she is still there, probably asleep. After that interesting update I asked Adolpha a very personal, helpful question.

"Why is your breath so minty?" I asked curiously.

"I put mint in my mouth to clean my teeth a bit," was her reply.

Whilst we were on the way to check on May we found out that Adolpha was a very tame wolf and she gets fed by a local farmer-woman called Hazel who loves animals and keeps and feeds them. Adolpha is basically her dog!

We woke up May and once we told her about Adolpha she walked into view.

We skipped off to Hazel's small cottage and as we were approaching her local field Adolpha told us about Charlotte (or Charlottie as she prefers to be called), Hazel's free-spirited, teenage granddaughter.

We were also told Charlotte means free-spirited too!

And apparently Hazel is pretty free-spirited herself - she tells off the local men and even broke up with her husband!!!

Unlike Mulberry farm, we weren't kept in pens and we were free to play in the huge field Hazel lives in.

Charlotte even loves to dance too! But she doesn't bother with ballet like all the other girls, instead she does a more 'free-spirited' style and really puts the emotion into it.

I know that I'll live a longer, happier life than most pigs but what can I say?

I'm a pig and I'm proud of it!

Lollipops and Rainbows

GENRE: FICTION: POETRY & RHYME

A Creation Poem:
How the Earth was Made

Written by Clare Ford,
Illustrated by Lillian Strickland

A star dropped into the ocean,

A moonbeam fell out of the sky,

Stardust mixed with sunlight,

A tear began to dry.

A soft rainbow made a light bridge,

A cloud transmitted a kind thought,

Lightning mixed with thunder,

The clouds began to part.

Sunlight cascaded through blackness,

Deep golden light felt soft, damp ground,

Silver drops covered vast seas,

Yellow sparks shone around.

SUGGESTED FOLLOW-UP ACTIVITIES

Curious Questions:

1. Discuss the creation of Earth. What stories and theories have you heard? What do you think about them and why?

2. Why do you think the human race has always been fascinated by creation stories? Compare and contrast a selection of creation stories from different cultures. Are there any similarities? If so, why? If not, why?

Aligned Activities:

1. Make a mind map of a creation poem. You can use your imagination or you can base your ideas on some of the themes you have discovered in Creation stories from different cultures, or a mixture of both your ideas and something you have read.
2. Re-write this play as a descriptive narrative.
3. Write your own story about magic events like Nelly and Emily have.

Magic Meditation:

Imagine sitting on the edge of another planet as you are watching the Earth being born.

A star dropped into the ocean – can you see it shimmer?

Hear it splash?

See it sink down to the bottom of the ocean…?

With your next in breath imagine inhaling the soft light from the moonbeam as you are standing on the rainbow bridge.

Look around at the beautiful points of starlight and know that you are connected to everything in the Universe.

That as you begin to really understand your place in this life time, you are supported by the Universe – by the clouds and the sunlight, by the rain and the thunder; that you are a being full of light.

Then, very slowly, wiggle your fingers and toes and come back to the room.

Magic Behind the Waterfall

Written by Emily Dowsett

It was a breezy summer's day and two friends, Zoe and Lilly, were playing in Zoe's garden on the swings. They were not sisters, but they were the best of friends and they looked alike. Zoe had long brown hair and usually wore it in two perfect braids. She wore a neat navy skirt and a crisp white top with a love heart logo. Lilly wore her brown hair in one neat braid with a similar blue skirt and a pink shiny top.

Both girls eventually got a little bit bored with playing on the swings and they decided to go for a calm walk in their local forest. The two young girls later found a waterfall. Zoe looked into the crystal-clear water, knowing that there must be some way to cross the river. Sure enough, large, cracked stepping stones caught Lilly's beautiful, sapphire eyes.

"Zoe, look!" Lily exclaimed. "There are some old cracked

stepping stones planted at the bottom of the water!" She showed them to Zoe and they jumped across them to the other side. When they got there, they saw a cave and Zoe wanted to go in but Lilly thought it was a bad idea because it was dark and eerie. Zoe ran to it and went inside. Of course, Lilly raced in after her and once she found her Lilly was just as amazed as Zoe.

They were standing in a magical unicorn land filled with pastel coloured unicorns. Both girls were shocked and speechless as they didn't think that unicorns were real. Instead of enjoying the moment, they just stood there with their mouths wide open.

Suddenly, one of the unicorns started to talk to them, she had a soft and gentle voice. Zoe and Lilly screamed out of fear but at the same time out of excitement. They replied with a simple 'hello'. The unicorn offered them a tour of their land and the girls followed her.

 "This is a great adventure," whispered Zoe to Lilly.

Towards the end of the day, the girls were playing with the unicorns having a great time. They had helped brush their manes and been rewarded by a ride on their backs. They had flown above the unicorn world and seen the magical features. But their fun was soon interrupted by an ear-piercing beeping sound and unicorns were running around chaotically.   The girls were scared that they may get trampled on. "What's happening?" asked Lilly.

"I don't know, let's go ask," replied Zoe.

Both girls walked over to the unicorn who had first greeted them when they arrived. She told them they needed their help to find a missing unicorn because their magic would be lost without every unicorn accounted for. One of the youngest unicorns, called Snow, had disappeared and not been seen for the day. "No magic?" shouted both girls in unison.

The girls took to the air without hesitation, on Sunshine and Waterfall, to search from the sky. The two unicorns searched across the land but Snow was nowhere to be seen.

After an hour they had to give up as the flight was exhausting and they needed a rest. Lilly had another idea, for them to visit the places Snow loved in the hope of finding her before the night came. The unicorns shared her favourite places and the girls went from one to another to look for her but returned empty-handed.

Finally, Cloud, the oldest unicorn in the land, remembered that all of the younger unicorns had trackers in their hoof bracelet for when they learned to fly alone. There was a small chance that Snow still had her bracelet on. They rushed to the Uni-library to search on the tracker device. Much to their relief, Snow still had her tracker in on her but it showed them that she was in desperate need of their help.

The flashing unicorn on the device showed that Snow was deep inside a dip in the mountainside. They didn't know what they would find when they got to Snow, so they packed some blankets and food along with some first aid equipment.

It was a quick journey to the mountain but Snow was hidden on the mountainside and it took some time to find her. When they did, they saw that she had a cut in her wing and she was very cold. They encouraged her to eat and used the blankets to warm her up. With all of their might, they managed to lift her out and get her to safety. They bandaged her wing and carried her to bed for some much-needed rest. She was very weak but she managed to whisper 'thank you'.

Lilly and Zoe stayed for a little while longer with their new friends, celebrating the safe return of Snow. They had a small tea party until it was time to return home themselves. The unicorns didn't want them to leave and they presented them both with a special locket filled with magical dust to revisit the Unicorn land whenever they wished. The girls made their way back to the cave and crossed the waterfall and found themselves back in the forest with Zoe's garden in the distance.

"Did that really happen?" Zoe questioned Lilly.

"Yes, what an amazing adventure, let's go back tomorrow."

Atlantica

Nelly, Amelia and the Vanishing Sea!

Written and Illustrated by Nelly E'beyer

Chapter 1

Many moons ago there was magic in the air, but bad magic! Balcazar was an old wizard that was not particularly good at spells and was always getting himself into lots of trouble. Balcazar lived

in a faraway seaside kingdom called Atlantica. Atlantica was a mysterious, hidden underground world full of mystical creatures. The seaside kingdom was an unusual but beautiful place to live, the sun always shone in the underground world and the birds were always singing.

Atlantica was so well hidden that no one other than the

people of Atlantica was able to find the secret entrance door which was in a cave on Shelly Beach.

Nelly and Amelia had lived in Atlantica their whole lives, they were sisters the best of friends and would do everything together.

They lived in a little teapot down Patchwork Lane with their mother and father and their pet dragon Zazu who was afraid of everything - even his own shadow!

Their grandfather, Balcazar, lived over the hill, up Wibbly Wobbly Lane in the tallest treehouse in Atlantica. Nelly and Amelia loved visiting their grandfather; he was the only wizard in the Kingdom.

The trouble was he was not a particularly good wizard, all his spells seemed to go wrong - he even managed to turn their parents into frogs!

Some people of Atlantica think he has been cursed by the naughty Hobknot that lives in Howling Woods.

Jester had been banished to the woods 200 years ago for bad behaviour - he had a nasty habit of freezing everything he touched and had not been seen since.

Chapter 2

Nelly and Amelia woke up bright and early one Saturday morning, to Zazu practising his fire skills. He had already burnt through half of the contents of their mother's sock drawer! Trying not to wake their parents they all silently crept out of the house. They ran as fast as they could all the way to their grandfather's house on the top of the hill.

Balcazar was busy bubbling up a spell. Green, gassy smoke had filled the air. The girls sensed there was big trouble ahead!

Balcazar shouted at the top of his lungs whilst frantically adding the ingredients into his cauldron.

"Frogs legs,

A pair of smelly socks,

Thorn from a rose,

An old dictionary,

Used teabag,

Feathers from crows."

The mixture bubbled and spat as he stirred the mixture round and round with his walking stick.

POP! BANG! WHIZZ! The spell exploded, Balcazar jumped back in surprise, bumping into Nelly and Amelia.

"Oh, hello girls, I didn't see you there. When did you arrive?" Balcazar asked, covered in green stinky goo!

"Morning grandfather, what spell are you conjuring up this time?" Nelly replied, in a concerned voice as she wiped the slime from her clothes. Zazu on the other hand was busy licking the goo up like it was ice cream.

"I found an amazing spell in my weekly magazine 'Magic For The Elderly'. I thought I would give it a try. But it seems to have gone wrong. Very strange as my spells always work… Now, where did I leave my spectacles?" Balcazar replied, baffled.

"Oh grandfather, your spells always go wrong!" Amelia exclaimed with a smirk on her face.

Balcazar chuckled "Girls you could just be right!"

Balcazar and the girls set to work cleaning up the mess. Zap the old Raven was busy squawking and flapping around trying to get their attention.

"Master, Master, squawk!!!"

"What now Zap, can't you see I'm busy?" Balcazar muttered.

"But Master, squawk, you have to look, the spell – it's leaking down into the village and, squawk, into the sea!" Zap replied frantically.

But it was no good, Balcazar ignored the Raven and carried on with his business. Soon it was the time for the girls and Zazu to leave, their parents would soon be wondering where they were.

As they reached the bottom of the rickety old wooden ladder, their faces dropped. The beautiful blue sea had vanished!!!

There was hardly anything left. Shocked fish were jumping around, the sea monster bridge that connected Atlantica to the Howling Woods was all that was left. Seashells covered the seabed and the green sticky goo glistened in the sun.

All the villagers heard the commotion and rushed out of their houses to be greeted by the dry land and the stench of the goo (which by the way smelt as bad as a rotten old egg!)

They all glared at the disaster that Balcazar had once again created.

What had he done!?

Chapter 3

Red faced and embarrassed, Balcazar hid his wand before slowly tip-toing backwards towards his treehouse. His shoulders hung low and he tried to make himself as small as he could so no one would see him. But it was too late. Officer Bronco pushed through the crowd to face the wizard (if you could call him that!)

"Balcazar, where do you think you're going? What is going on here?

Balcazar (looking redder than ever) quietly replied "Umm, I may have had a bit of an accident, nothing to worry about, I'm sure I can fix this!"

"You think you can fix this disaster?" screamed Officer Bronco.

"Umm well I think I can, if I just pop home and have a look in my trusty spell book, I'm sure I can find something." Balcazar said brightly.

"Noooooooo!" shouted the whole of Atlantica.

Nelly and Amelia stepped forward to help their grandfather.

"PC Bronco let us help to get the sea back, we will find a way!"

Chapter 4

The girls had promised the whole entire Kingdom that they would find a spell to bring back the seas plug and turn the mountain tap on. But now they had to figure out how they would find it!

"Hello Ozzy, what brings you here?" said Amelia.

Ozzy was a mean little Oobertrom that lived under Crystal Falls on the East, West, North, South and slightly to the right of the Island. Ozzy was no bigger than a chihuahua but was just as snappy.

"Well, I had heard that you were in topsy turvy trouble and I thought I would come to your rescue," the little Oobertrom sniggered.

Lollipops and Rainbows

"You want to help us? You have never helped anyone before, what are you up to Ozzy?" asked Amelia suspiciously.

"Now let's not be hasty, if I tell you where to find the spell that will bring your glorious sea back then perhaps you can do something for me? All I want in return is to be granted one spell from Balcazar."

Nelly and Amelia were not happy about this, but they decided they had no choice.

"Ok Ozzy it's a deal." Amelia agreed.

Ozzy told them that they had to make their way to Howling Woods to see Jester the banished Hobknot who would have the spell they needed. He warned them of the flying wolves and the whispering trees. And under no circumstances should they speak to the troll tribe that lived amongst the shrubs.

"Grif here will take you to the entrance of the woods, but after that you're on your own." explained Ozzy.

Grif swooped down for the girls to jump aboard. Nelly and Amelia nervously climbed up onto the Griffins back and held on tight.

Lollipops and Rainbows

"Good luck!" Ozzy sniggered.

Grif soared up into the blue sky, and off they went on their adventure.

They soon arrived at Howling Wood, where Grif dropped them to the ground.

"Sorry kids, I can't come any further, it's not safe." and with that she was gone.

It had suddenly turned dark and grey. Fog and mist had filled the air. And a howling noise screeched through the air. Nelly and Amelia looked at each other "Flying wolves!" The girls hid behind the trees until it was safe to come out. As they started to venture further into the fog, the trees rustled and whispered in their ears. The girls did not like this place, they felt like they were being watched.

As they walked ahead there was a clearing, a little door on a tree stood in front of them. Should they knock? Or should they walk the other way? Nelly and Amelia decided to be brave and knock on the little door. They held their breath as they waited to see what or who would greet them.

The door creaked open to reveal Jester the banished Hobknot wearing thick brown gloves and a green scruffy outfit.

"WhaTT do youS two want of me, why youS disturbed me, I'm buSY" Jester spat.

Lollipops and Rainbows

"Sorry to bother you, but we really need your help. Ozzy told us you had a spell that we need. The Sea has disappeared and we need the spell to bring it back." Nelly explained desperately.

"WhY should me hElp youS, youS banished me all here yeerS ago." he replied.

"We're sorry, but that was a long time ago and had nothing to do with us. Please help us and we will ask the Mayor Donald Trout to allow you to return." Amelia pleaded.

Jester thought long and hard.

"OK, inS youS come whilst I find the spell youS are lookin for." said Jester.

The girls followed the Hobknot into his little house in the tree. It was the strangest house they had ever seen. Everything was upside down, the ceiling was on the floor, the furniture was on the ceiling. Everything was all in a muddle.

Jester rummaged around in his cupboards and pulled out a big jar full of old papers. He reached inside and extracted the spell that the girls needed.

"Here go youS, here is the spEll that will plug the seE and turnS onS the mountin tAps."

The girls smiled and thanked Jester before they all made their way back to Atlantica.

Chapter 5

When they arrived, the people of Atlantica came out to greet them from their quest. They were shocked to see Jester the Hobknot with them. PC Bronco once again bounced through the crowd with his large belly.

"Great Scots what is HE doing here?" he blared out.

Jester frowned.

"PC Bronco, Jester is not a bad little Hobknot, it's not his fault. He has magical powers within his hands that makes him turn things to ice. Look, that is why he now wears gloves. We think he should be allowed to return to Atlantica where he belongs." Nelly pleaded.

Jester stood forward to show the crowd his gloved hands.

Donald Trout jumped up and down in the dry sea.

"Nice to see you old friend - as long as those gloves stay firmly on and you promise to not turn anything to ice, you can remain in Atlantica. Maybe you could be of use to the City and help keep out any bad enemies," The Mayor declared.

Nelly, Amelia and Jester cheered and jumped for joy. But there was still one last thing to do. They handed the spell over to Balcazar.

"Eyeballs,

Ice burgs,

Old Lady's Shawl,

Dragon's Tail,

A Humpback Whale,

Plug the sea and turn on the mountain tap,

One last thing 15 swimming caps."

CABOOOOOOOOOOOMMMMMM!

The air filled with blue smoke as the mountain tap turned on and started to fill the sea with fresh blue water.

Everyone cheered and clapped, the girls had done it!

To celebrate the town had a street party, balloons and fireworks filled the air as the people of Atlantica partied the night away.

Nelly and Amelia yawned and decided to make their way back home. On their way, they passed their grandfather's treehouse and spotted Ozzy and Balcazar around the cauldron, green smoke filling the air around the treehouse…

"Oh no, here we go again!!!!...

GENRE: NON-FICTION: INSTRUCTIONAL WRITING

A Recipe for Sunshine

Written by Clare Ford,
Illustrated by Dóireann Cahill

You will need:

- A sprinkle of smiles
- A pint of peace
- A cup of kisses
- A handful of healing
- A touch of tickles
- A colander of cuddles
- A kilo of kindness
- A litre of laughter
- A spoonful of stardust
- A helping hand
- A whole lot of love
- A bowl
- A mixing spoon

Instructions:

1. First, take your bowl and a mixing spoon.
2. Next, add the peace, cuddles and kindness, and fold until soft.
3. Then, add the kisses and laughter, with a helping hand and love.
4. Finally, sprinkle smiles, tickles and stardust

5. Now you have your very own bowl of sunshine and happiness to share.

Illustrated by Dóireann Cahill

SUGGESTED FOLLOW-UP ACTIVITIES

Curious Questions:

1. Are there any ingredients that might be missing from the recipe that you would want to add? Why? Why is that important?
2. Can you find the imperative (bossy) verbs in each instruction?
3. What are the time connectives that have been used at the start of each sentence?

Aligned Activities:

1. Make a list of all the things you do that make you happy. Now can you think of 5 more?
2. Create your own recipe for happiness
3. Paint a sunset picture, like Nelly has.
4. Create an explanation leaflet of how the heart works.
5. Go outside and celebrate the life-giving rays of the sun like Dóireann has.

Dóireann and Sunshine enjoying the Sunshine

"Sunset" Illustrated by Nelly E'beyer

Magic Meditation:

Imagine sitting on a beautiful sandy beach, gazing out over the still turquoise water.

Turn to watch the sun as it begins its descent into the ocean, filling the sky with a myriad of different colours, including burnt orange, pale yellow, lime green, magenta pink, indigo and violet. Immerse yourself in these beautiful colours of the sunset; breathing them into your body and breathing out white sparkly light.

Know that you are a Spirit of the Light and that your love shines out into the world. Now imagine being on the beach with a person you are very close to and love dearly. Imagine holding hands with them and walking together along the beach. Breathe in the feelings of love, calm and peace, into your heart. And send breathe these feelings out into the world around you.

Then, very slowly, wiggle your fingers and toes and come back to the room.

Lollipops and Rainbows

GENRE: NON- FICTION: LETTER WRITING

A Letter to my Heart

Written by Clare Ford

111 Galaxy Drive
Moonbeam City
Stellar Island
PS24 9JW
The Universe

22nd April 10 years from now

Mrs Heart
22 Love Drive
Milky Way
37X 5YD
The Universe

Dear Mrs Heart,
Reference: Better Times Are Coming

I am writing to you with words of encouragement in the hope that you will feel better soon.
I know that you are hurting and that sometimes you feel

bruised… Just know that I will try to protect you from breaking.

I must remember to fill you up with pink, sparkly light every day, so that the darkness has no place to go.

When you are overflowing with light then together we can send this positive light out into the world and to the people surrounding us.

When you are overflowing with light then together we can send love out into nature – to the trees, oceans and animals that are surrounding us.

When you are overflowing with light then together we can send this positive light out into the Universe – to every star and moonbeam surrounding us. Together, we can heal the world.

Thank you for taking the time to read this letter. Please do not hesitate to connect with me if you have any further questions.

Kindest Regards,

Me x

SUGGESTED FOLLOW-UP ACTIVITIES

Curious Questions:

1. How does it feel to have your heart broken? What happened?
2. How would you mend a broken heart if you had access to any medicine in the Universe?

Aligned Activities:

1. Write a letter to a real or an imaginary friend about a happy or sad event in your life
2. Make a collage or draw a picture of a heart using paper and sparkles
3. Write a story about a real or imagined sad or strange event, like Ellie has.

Magic Meditation:

Imagine sitting at the very top of the world, in a peaceful, safe place.

Put your hand over your heart.

Start breathing in slowly, pausing and then breathing out slowly.

As your breath slows, send your attention to your heart chakra. Inhale pink sparkly light through your nose and send it into your heart until it overflows... then send it everywhere around your body.

Now inhale and exhale pale green light and send this out to the four corners of the world. Repeat and this time send the light further, to the far reaches of the Universe.

Now imagine you are sitting in a beautiful, pale pink bubble of light where you a protected and no blackness can seep through.

Then, very slowly, wiggle your fingers and toes and come back to the room.

The Planet of Mortals and Mystics

Written by Ellie Clements

(Hi! I am the narrator, I tell the story, anything that does not have speech marks is me!! Anyway, let us start the story!)

It was midnight in this world, the sky was dark and not a star could be seen. Right now, three friends, Kitty, Megan and Shane are awake talking about what will happen tomorrow, but little did they know that tomorrow would not be like they thought...

The next day, the children woke up, checked the time - it was 10:00am but when they looked out the window it was pitch black with just a few twinkles of bright light coming from the stars. It looked like it was still midnight; they ran downstairs to look at the time on their giant, wooden clock, but it said the exact same as their phones! Two hours' later, Megan went outside to get lunch from the outdoor fridge, but it was still pitch black.

'The stars have disappeared! They were out earlier!!' called Megan.

The friends were very confused.

'Oh no! Should I find my wand?' asked Kitty.

'Of course you should!" shouted Shane from inside their small cottage in the enchanted woods.

Half an hour later, Kitty finally found her wand and cast a spell to call the Alpha Wolf.

When she got to Kitty, The Alpha Wolf asked her what they needed her for, and she explained, 'The stars have disappeared!'

'That's terrible!' exclaimed the Alpha 'So, what can I do?'

'Well, I know you have found stars before, so I thought you might be able to help?' guessed Kitty.

'Well... I guess I can try,' said the Alpha.

'I hope she can,' thought Kitty.

'I read your mind!' whispered Megan to Kitty.

'Stop it, stop it!!' thought Kitty

'Oh no... Now we have two problems to sort out...' mumbled Shane.

'What do you mean?' asked The Alpha.

'Megan and Kitty are arguing, and the stars have disappeared!!!' replied Shane.

A few hours later, something amazing happened.

They had figured out one of the problems!

'WE NEED TO FIND THE STARS BEFORE THEY ARE GONE FOREVER!' interrupted Megan.

They headed to the wolves' cave.

'No, our tree...' mumbled Kitty.

'What do you mean?' said Megan.

'I-it is gone.... It's been chopped down.' explained Kitty.

'RUN!!' shouted Shane

They ran.

'WHY?!' Megan yelled.

'THE HUNTERS!! THEY ARE HERE FOR OUR POWERS!!!!' screamed Kitty, peering anxiously behind her.

None of them had super speed... but then Kitty remembered something.

'I can swim like a mermaid.... I CAN SWIM LIKE A MERMAID!!! Run to the beach.' shouted Kitty excitedly.

They ran VERY quickly to the beach. When they got there Megan and Shane got into the boat, Kitty grabbed a rope, tied it to the front of the boat and around her waist.

She swam and swam.

'Phew, I am exhausted!' said Kitty.

'Oh my! Is that an island?!'

And it was.

'Oh! It is! Try to get there!' said Shane. 'Quickly! I am starving!'

'Ok, I will find food, you can make weapons and Megan you can make shelter!' decided Kitty.

When they got to the island, they saw three bears.

One looked like a polar bear; another looked like a brown bear, but the other looked very strange and was grey.

Kitty tried to talk to them, but she couldn't understand them.

'Weird... I can't understand them...' said Kitty.

Were they friendly or not?

Lollipops and Rainbows

GENRE: FICTION: STORY WRITING BASED ON A TRADITIONAL TALE

The Swan's Song

Adapted by Clare Ford

This is a story about a swan…. Or should I say a rather strange grey fluffy looking bird who didn't fit in anywhere.

As you probably know, the little cygnet was looked after by a mother duck and its brothers and sisters were the baby ducklings in the family. Needless to say, the cygnet could neither move nor swim with the same grace and ease as the ducklings, and began to feel very out of place. It was much larger than its yellow, fluffy siblings and was very clumsy. The ducklings began to tease the cygnet, out of ear shot of their mother, of course – and the cygnet felt lonely and sad and different.

One early morning, our grey fluffy friend set off, head down, to live elsewhere. Passing a near-by farm, the cygnet approached the resident sheep dog, to make a new friend. But it barked loudly and bared its canine teeth and the cygnet was afraid…

As it turned to run, the farmyard geese gave chase too and the cygnet felt even more unhappy and alone.

After spending a cold and uncomfortable night in a bed of straw shared with mice, the cygnet set off again the next day. It shook and stretched and noticed some soft, grey feathers floating to the ground as it did so. As the sun began to rise, the cygnet plucked up courage and moved on... wondering why it didn't fit in – wondering why it looked so different and moved in such a clumsy way; wondering why it had no family to belong to.

Eventually, stopping at a small pond to drink, the cygnet noticed a large tear plop into the water. It looked closer and after a brief minute of surprise realised it belonged to him... The reason the cygnet was surprised was because it no longer resembled the grey, fluffy ungainly animal from a few weeks earlier.

The cygnet had turned into a beautiful swan at last... And, as it gazed disbelievingly into the pond, the swan saw a flock of white birds reflected in the sky above. "Wow! It thought to itself – those birds look so gracious... They are flying with such ease and they are so white – they look majestic against the blue sky."

Unbelievably, the flock of swans were flying towards the pond, and landed gracefully nearby. One of the swans approached our friend and said, "We have been looking everywhere for you. It's time for you to come and fly away with us. We are your family." As the swan felt another large tear roll down its white cheek, it let out a sigh of relief.

"Well, what are you waiting for?" asked the main swan.

"You can fly; you can swim. Let us show you the beautiful lake where we live."

And, after a few tentative steps, the beautiful flock of swans set off, flying high in the sky, their wings dipped in the pale pick glow of the setting sun.

SUGGESTED FOLLOW-UP ACTIVITIES

Curious Questions:

Why do you think the title of the story is the Swan Song? What is there to sing about? What is there to celebrate?

1. Do you sometimes feel isolated from your family and friends? If this has happened, how have you overcome your feelings?
2. What do you think the moral of this story really is?
3. Everybody is beautiful on the inside... Discuss.
4. What traditional tale is this story based on? Why do you think these stories stand the test of time?
5.

Aligned Activities:

1. Make a mind-map about yourself; listing all your beautiful qualities, skills, attributes; your family, friends and pets; any clubs or activities you take part in... use different colours and allow the mind-map to

grow as big as you like. You can add to it at any time.

2. Write a powerful message to yourself on the bathroom mirror so you see it when you brush your teeth.

3. Choose any of these statements, write them in the middle of a postcard and then decorate and frame them. Put them up somewhere in your bedroom where you will see them every day.
"I AM ME. I AM BEAUTIFUL. I AM STRONG. I AM UNIQUE." like Oskar has.

4. Turn this story, or your favourite traditional tale, into a narrative poem.

5. Write a story about how things are not always what they seem, like Emilia has.

Designed by Oskar Ford

Magic Meditation:

Imagine sitting at the edge of a very beautiful and peaceful lake... feel the green grass tickle your toes and the soles of your feet... feel the warm sun on your face and a slight breeze coming off the lake tickle the hairs on your arms.

You take a deep breath in and the out, slowly. And again.

And with each breath, feel any anxiety slipping away. Every time you breathe out, let go of any anxiety – worry about not being like your friends; let go of worry about not getting on with people in your family.

With each in-breath, say to yourself "I am loved."

With each out-breath, say to yourself, "I am love."

And now, fill your body with white sparkly light of peace and love of the universe...

Once your body is full of this light, imagine in your mind's eye that you lean over to scoop some of the cold, fresh water from the lake into your hand.

And as you do so, notice your reflection in the water... slightly distorted from the ripples at first.

Then, as the water clears, you can see yourself more distinctly. And you notice how the light shines from inside you. How your heart is filled with joy.

How you are radiant and shining and beautiful....

And you may just feel a tear roll down your soft cheek, because now you know for sure that you are holding the secret of the Universe in your hand; in that pure cold water, is the reflection of everything – everything including the radiance and beauty that is in your soul and the purity that is in your spirit.

Then, very slowly, wiggle your fingers and toes and come back to the room.

Detective Darcie and the Missing Doughnuts

Written and Illustrated by Emilia Catanach

The rooster crowed as the first glimpse of sun peeked over the horizon, casting a warm orange glow over Tiny Town. The dawn chorus grew louder as the birds slowly awoke from their slumber. Cats slunk in the shadows as the streets started to come alive with people going about their day.

In the middle of town, at world famous Baguette's Bakery, Mr. Baguette, the baker, was already hard at work preparing a fresh batch of doughnuts, his most sought-after treat. A queue had already started to form outside his shop, with many beady eyes eyeing up the iced glazed doughnuts on show.

The sickly-sweet sugary smell wafted through the air.

The queue stretched for miles. Everyone was waiting for the doors to open. Suddenly, there was a loud crash. All eyes darted towards the sound as a rickety lorry roared past.

But when their heads turned back to the bakery window, all the doughnuts had VANISHED!

Just down the road, Detective Darcie was busy putting her Super Sleuth clothes, hat and gloves on when her phone rang. It was Mr. Baguette. He sounded alarmed.

"ARGH!!! HELP! HELP! MY DOUGHNUTS HAVE GONE MISSING!"

Detective Darcie ran out of the house, jumped on her motorbike and sped into town.

When she arrived at Baguette's Bakery, she was met by an angry mob demanding to know where the doughnuts had gone. Mr. Baguette scratched his head. He looked puzzled. Hmmmm, thought the Detective, rubbing her chin. Suspicious … very suspicious indeed. She sniffed the air. There was a hint of something sweet. Cinnamon perhaps. She took out her magnifying glass and, with her twitchy nose in the air, started to follow the trail.

First stop was Mrs. Sugarlump's cottage. She was always buying sugar from the bakery to go with her steaming hot tea. Maybe today she'd decided to take the doughnuts too! Yes, it had to be her! Detective Darcie peered through her magnifying glass … only to find that there wasn't a trail. No doughnut crumbs or grains of sugar could be found!

Next stop was Billy Brown, the town bully. He was always stealing sweets and chocolates from smaller children so was bound to be the culprit. Yet, on closer inspection, he too was innocent.

Drat, thought Detective Darcie. She peered around her and saw something shimmering on the ground.

It was leading to Jemima Jelly's house. Of course, she thought. And set off to confront her.

Jemima Jelly was busy in her kitchen making fairy cakes and sprinkling them with every coloured sprinkle imaginable. She was a very messy baker so the sprinkles were EVERYWHERE ... and sparkling in the sunlight. It wasn't the right trail, after all.

Detective Darcie was puzzled. All the usual suspects were innocent! There was only one thing for it – she had to go to speak to the town mascot, a giant life-sized, walking, talking, sugar-coated jelly baby. He knew all the goings on in Tiny Town.

The mascot sat at his usual spot in the park. Detective Darcie sauntered over to him. "I'm having trouble solving the case of the missing doughnuts," she said. "What do you think I should do?"

The mascot, without turning to look at her, said wisely, "Go back to where it began."

Detective Darcie was even more confused. What did he mean? Go back to the bakery? But hadn't she already investigated there? However, she did as she was told, jumped on her motorbike again, and sped back into town.

Mr. Baguette was serving his last customer for the day when Detective Darcie burst in, feeling confused. She looked around her. Everything looked the same as it had before... yet different somehow. It was like she was seeing everything through new, fresh eyes. She knew the clues were right under her nose. She just had to find them.

Lollipops and Rainbows

Glancing around, she took a closer look at Mr. Baguette. He was waiting to close the shop and looking very sheepish. Something in Detective Darcie's gut told her that things weren't quite as they seemed. She peered at his hair, which this morning looked like its typical brown and frizzy mess. But when she looked closer, there was something in it. Something that glistened. She looked at his moustache. It looked sticky. She looked directly into Mr. Baguette's eyes. They started to water as if he were about to cry.

"I'm so sorry," he said, "it was me. I ate the doughnuts. They were so delicious. I couldn't resist. So, while no one was looking, I ate them all. And instead of owning up, I lied and said they'd been stolen." He burst into tears.

Detective Darcie looked at him in surprise. She had blamed Mrs. Sugarlump, Billy Brown the town bully, and Jemima Jelly when it was the baker all along.

Detective Darcie disappeared into the kitchen and, a few minutes later, returned with a hot mug of cocoa with whipped cream and marshmallows. She passed it to Mr. Baguette.

"Lying is not okay. A single lie can hurt many people," she said, with a warm smile. "But we all make mistakes. What you do now is what counts."

Mr. Baguette felt immense gratitude towards Detective Darcie. She was right, lying was not okay, and now he had a chance to make amends.

The following morning, as the rooster crowed and the birds burst into song, quite a crowd was gathering outside Mr. Baguette's bakery. Music could be heard blaring from the kitchen and colourful balloons and banners adorned the shop windows. Inside, Mr. Baguette was getting ready for opening time. He'd been up all night baking his best recipes for Tiny Town to enjoy.

"Doughnuts are on me," he cried as he opened the doors. Never would Mr. Baguette lie again.

And never again would Detective Darcie jump to conclusions without having all the facts first!

A Song for Humanity

Written by Clare Ford

Gaia Earth, Gaia Earth, mother and nurturer
Father Sky, Father Sky, guide and protector

Open up my heart; surrender to love,
Open up my voice and hear my heart sing,
Open up my eyes and see my true self,
Open my heart for the light to flood in.

Gaia Earth, Gaia Earth, mother and nurturer
Father Sky, Father Sky, guide and protector

See our Universe gently pulsating,
Hear sweet birdsong and gentle rain falling,
Sense my star fam'ly sparkling and twinkling,
Taste hot winds shifting, cool waters soothing.

Gaia Earth, Gaia Earth, mother and nurturer
Father Sky, Father Sky, guide and protector

Beautiful light of the Ancients to guide us,
Wisdom and courage available to us,
Feelings of peace and contentment inside us,
The whole world in harm'ny, singing with us.

Gaia Earth, Gaia Earth, mother and nurturer
Father Sky, Father Sky, guide and protector

SUGGESTED FOLLOW-UP ACTIVITIES

Curious Questions:

1. How does this song make you feel?
2. Which lyrics appeal to you most? Why?

Aligned Activities:

1. Write the next verse to the song
2. Count the number of syllables in each line and continue the pattern
3. Design a CD cover for the song, like Nelly has.
4. Sing the song to your own music and drum along
5. Investigate Shamanic and Tribal songs from different cultures
6. Write a story about the power of Nature, like Tomás has.

A Song for Humanity CD cover designed by Nelly E'beyer

Lollipops and Rainbows

Magic Meditation:

Imagine sitting on the top of a mountain with the guardians of the Earth and Universe and the Angels all around you, singing this song.

Imagine opening your heart and with each in breath fill it with feelings of love.

Imagine everyone on the planet linking hands to make a circle of love, singing the chorus together.

Take a deep breath in, and when you breathe out, breathe out sparkly white light to the furthest corners of the earth and to the far reaches of the Universe.

Know that you are in harmony with the Universe.

Then, very slowly, wiggle your fingers and toes and come back to the room.

What Lurks Within the Temple?

Written by Tomás Cahill

Mr. Big Ears is no ordinary rabbit, he is the leader of Planet Nibbles.

Planet Nibbles is home to a very sacred temple which the rabbits of planet Nibble worship. You see the temple has a unique energy source which provides an earth-like atmosphere for its residents. This temple is the envy of other planets such as Planet Woogoo.

Woogoo is home to a species of fox. They have lived together in harmony for as long as we remember - until now!!

The Woogarians have grown tired of their bulky space suits (just try imagine a fox scampering around in a SPACE SUIT!) they long for their freedom to roam and do as they like, just as the Rabbits of Nibbles do.

This is where animal instincts take over!

Mr. Big Ears, being a creature of habit, whilst out foraging, stumbled across a large boulder blocking his usual path. Strange and on investigation, he noticed some unusual markings on the stone. He had seen these markings before... "THE TEMPLE!!" he thought.

He ran as fast as he could to the camp to tell the others. Exhausted, he reached the camp. All the Nibbles had gone, the camp intact but there was evidence of a struggle, burrows damaged, vegetable suppers simmering, the playground deserted, alone he could only think of one thing - GO TO THE TEMPLE!!

Mr. Big Ears reached the temple...immediately he was taken by several Woogarians towards their leader "SLY". He could not believe his eyes. SLY and his Woogarians were dismantling the temple boulder by boulder. The same boulders he'd seen on his walk earlier. "They are here to steal the Temple" Mr. Big Ears thought. The other Nibbles were being held captive crying on their knees as they pointed to the temple in disbelief!! Thankfully they were unharmed, but the rabbits were powerless to do anything.

Mr. Big Ears tried to reason with SLY, but he did not want to listen. Quickly MR Big Ears hopped onto the boulder that SLY had in his grip. The markings on the boulder suddenly glowed with a bright light which had never been seen before. The light reflected paw prints of Rabbits and Foxes side by side.

Suddenly, the Temple began to transform and a bright silhouette appeared from it... "I'm MOTHER NATURE" she called out in the sweetest voice. Both Mr. Big Ears and SLY dropped to their knees together as if they were one, with that the Nibbles were set free and there was a sense of calm between the animals.

Mother Nature stepped forward in all her beauty and offered an easy solution where they live together in harmony on Planet Nibbles. The Woogarians all cheered as they could finally run, skip, and jump without spacesuits in this special place. They worked together to rebuild the temple and cherish it together.

Who Am I?

Written by Clare Ford

Hello and good day. Who is this person that you see sitting in front of you today?

Well. I'll start with my name, Clare, which means light and bright and clear, derived from the Latin term "clarus", and the Medieval name Clara. You'll have to decide if my name fits!

Who am I? Let's start off with definitions to do with relationships...

I am a mother of two teenage boys, a daughter, a sister, an aunty, a step-grandmother, an ex-wife and a partner... A survivor of depression and anxiety.

Does that really help you get a sense of Who I AM? Or actually are these just labels? So often we define ourselves by the people who are in our lives. The people and the circumstances that happen to us aren't necessarily the definition that we need to have. We are more than our circumstances!

So, let's strip away that layer of the onion and go a little bit deeper...

Let's think again... Who Am I?

Some people might resonate with this definition...

A Piscean with rising Leo, Numerology Life Path 7; Pleiadean Indigo Star seed....

No – it doesn't necessarily mean a lot to everybody, although these are still definitions that some people find extremely important and interesting and take very seriously indeed. But actually, these are also just labels so we need to peel away that layer of the onion too...

Let's delve a bit deeper now. Who Am I?

I am a compassionate, caring, intelligent person who likes to help people reach their full potential. This is why I have been a teacher for 15 years; I am now a private tutor and a qualified transformational life coach and energy healer.

Is that getting closer to the essence of who I am? Well, it tells us about what I do and why I do it... But actually, lots of people may be like that. So, what is it that makes us uniquely who we are? What is it that makes me uniquely different from other caring, compassionate, intelligent, wonderful life coaches, healers and teachers?

I have, in my life, undergone some very difficult situations and circumstances, to the extent that the flame inside of me was nearly extinguished. So, I'm now going to define myself like this:

I am a person who is stepping out of the darkness; who is stepping into her power; who is reaching the light; is stepping up, taking responsibility and fulfilling her true life purpose. Now that is beginning to resonate with me.

I am not defining myself by the circumstances that have happened to me in the past. But would I choose to change those things? No, I wouldn't. If I hadn't been in those dark places in my life, I would not have built up the resilience, understanding and knowledge; the enlightenment, the drive, the power and the determination that is within me.

And this is how we begin to transform ourselves.

This is how we step into the true essence of who we are.

By shedding our skin. By peeling away the layers. By putting aside, the labels. By putting aside, the circumstances.

They have happened to us. We are those things to other people. But we do not have to define ourselves by those things.

We actually have a choice.

And I choose to be the person to serve others so that they too can understand their true life purpose.

I choose to be courageous enough to be ME!

It is my weaknesses that make me strong and my imperfections that make me beautiful.

I choose to shine my light.

I choose to be CLARE.

So, who are you?

What do you choose?

SUGGESTED FOLLOW-UP ACTIVITIES

Curious Questions:

1. Why is it important to have a strong sense of "self"?
2. Are other people's opinions about you important? Discuss. Write a story about this like Scarlett has.
3. What do the words "Life Purpose" mean to you?

Aligned Activities:

1. Find out about the meaning and derivation of your name. Do you think it suits you?

2. Write a description of yourself... think of starting with the outer layers – your relationships; family; hobbies; favourite subjects; then think more about your strengths and gifts – what makes you a special and wonderful person? How do you help and inspire other people? Perhaps you could write a diary entry like Fedora has.

3. Interview an adult who you know well and ask them "Who are you?"; "How would you describe yourself?" Make notes and turn your interview into a character description.

Magic Meditation:

Take a deep breath in and imagine that you are drifting in space, amongst the stars.

With each inhalation and exhalation, let yourself drift further still, knowing that you are perfectly safe.

As you become used to your new surroundings, you see a myriad of colours and lights; beautiful, sparkling, reflecting.

You smile to yourself because you know that you too are starlight.

You know that you are moonbeams.

You know that you are every particle of light - that you are made of light.

That you are light.

Once you know this, then you need not be afraid.

For you are light and love.

And this is your gift.

As you spend time floating among the stars, you find your star seed and your galactic family.

You realise that there are many light beings, just like you.

Slowly, very slowly, you bring yourself back, floating back down with every breath, feeling heavier now as you come back into the room.

Then, very slowly, wiggle your fingers and toes and open your eyes.

Threat to Teddy Mountain

Written and Illustrated by Scarlett Hodder

The mountain had always stood majestically in the centre of Teddy Island. It was beautiful, with a shimmering waterfall running down the side leading to a fast-flowing river that sparkled in the sunshine, that always seemed to shine on the mountain side.

Out of the blue, some rocks descended quickly to the base of the mountain, the humongous hill felt like there was an earthquake and was shaking like trees caught in a tornado.

At the foot of the mountain, hidden behind the waterfall was a tiny, secret hole; people passing by would never notice the small entrance, but all the teddies on the island knew it was there, as it was actually an entrance to a cave that led all the way to the top of the mountain, where there was a miniscule viewing platform.

This is where the teddies called Home.

The cave was a massive place, with lots of green bushes which were full of different types of the bears' favourite berries and bowls of rainbow candy canes. All the bears felt it was such a friendly and happy place to live. All around there were many party rooms, always playing music, which made the bears feel excited. Each teddy had their own bedroom, but there was one empty room! This room used to belong to Mr. Happy Bear, though these days he calls himself Mr. Heartbroken Bear!

Mr. Heartbroken Bear used to be part of the teddy team, but he ran away after he thought he'd wrecked the Princess' party. The parties that the princess threw were always amazing, with freshly picked berries and candy canes, and lots of new bears coming to join the fun; there were disco balls which were shiny and glistened in the moonlight, that shone down through the viewing platform. At one party Mr. Happy Bear had more candy canes than were allowed and had an immense sugar rush which made him climb up on one of the tables and swing on one of the disco balls, like a monkey dangling from a tree!

Everybody looked.

Everybody dropped their cups while looking in shock at the unexpected sight!

"Get down right now!!!" bawled Princess Cuties' guards, "Or the disco ball will… " The guards were interrupted by a colossal crash, as the disco ball fell to the floor. Mr. Happy Bear felt very sad, his sugar rush concluded abruptly, he was very embarrassed and ran away as quick as his bouncing legs could carry him. Princess Cutie felt so blue for the depressed bear that she sent her guards straight after him so she could say it was ok because it wasn't really his fault as he just ate a bit too much of his favourite food.

As Mr. Happy Bear was running away, he turned and saw the guards chasing after him. Mr. Bear thought the guards wanted to take him to teddy jail, so he ran even faster and climbed to the top of the mountain!

The bear ran faster. The guards slowed down. Very soon the guards gave up and returned to the party to give Princess Cutie the unpleasant news.

When Mr. Bear realised the guards had turned around and given up on him, he thought that no one cared about him! This made him feel very dejected!

Mr. Bear lived near the top of the mountain for nearly two years, living off the lovely berry bushes, every day feeling more and more tearful until one day he turned from Mr. Happy Bear to Mr. Heartbroken Bear!

"Why should I have ever trusted all those bears?" he thought, not realising that further down the mountain, Princess Cuties guards were out looking for him every single day. His tears dropped like rain and after such a long time all the extra tears in the river was putting too much pressure on the rocks near the edge of the waterfall.

RUMBLE!

CRASH!

The water crashing became louder every day until there was a crash that was louder than any other and the rocks began to rain down, covering the entrance to the cave!!

Quickly Mr. Bear climbed down the mountain as fast as a mountain cheetah going to catch its prey! Within seconds he arrived at the base of the mountain and tried to move the still falling rocks. For two hours' he worked as hard as he could, but he began to feel weary and dizzy and decided to have a little sit down and a break. Within a few seconds he was asleep but was woken suddenly by an alarming noise!

WHOOSH!! The noise was rocks being thrown away at breakneck speed, away from the cave entrance!

"Is that a banana???" Mr. Bear thought out loud……

"YES!" Shouted the passing flash of yellow. Before Mr. Bear could answer he heard someone shout his name. He turned around and saw Princess Cutie running towards him! He felt a little bit scared but before he could run again, she hugged him tight.

"I was very worried Mr. Bear; I have not seen you in years." she cried.

"Sorry about what happened," said Mr. Bear "I did not mean to push the rocks down, it was my tears!!"

"Why were you crying?" she asked.

"I thought no one cared about me," he said sadly, "and I am so sorry for what happened."

"It's ok, let's just put it right." she answered kindly.

They turned back to the entrance to the cave to start work but surprisingly it was already cleared!!

Sitting relaxing near the entrance were Superteddy and his sidekick Bananaguy!! Mr. Bear could not believe that the rumours were true - there were superheroes on Teddy Island!!

"Hi friends!" Princess Cutie said casually. "Thanks for rescuing the teddies, who were running around the fields shouting, "I'm free!!!"

As Mr. Bear and Princess Cutie watched the bears, they laughed and ran to join in the fun! Superteddy and Bananaguy joined in as well, doing funny dances, when they suddenly stopped.

Bananaguy's super hearing told them that far away there was a cry for help and as quick as a flash off they flew!!

Daisy's Diary:
A Girl Scouts Adventure

Written and Illustrated by Fedora Mensah

Dear Diary,

Today, I was more lost than ever. One minute I was holding hands with my best friend, Liz from my Girl Scouts team as we were going on an expedition in the Mongudasi Forests. Then, curiosity got the best out of me when I spotted a stunning, rare butterfly, left hands with Liz and went over to touch it.

When I turned back around, I realised I had been left behind. Trembling, I entered the completely damp forest. I was entranced by the dense trees in a thick canopy, calmingly closing in on me; it is a different view from life in the city.

Serpents of smoke surrounded my nose as I kept walking.

Feeling cold and frightened immediately, I sniffed back my silent, shuddering sobs secretly. There was an uneasy, gripping pain in my heart.

It was one miserable adventure as I trudged sadly, missing my friends. Something kept warning me not to continue but at the same time I felt like I should keep going.

Which voice would you have listened to?

One, two, three thick droplets of rain hit me hard on the head, drenching my Girl Scouts uniform. Once the first tear had broken loose, the others followed in an unbroken stream.

The sun was gradually disappearing, and darkness was creeping in slowly but surely. I found it harder to find my way. My ears listened carefully to the voices of the dark and night creatures. Suddenly, it felt like someone or something was watching me.

"Aargh! Help! Liz? Miss Kelly?" I cried but there was no response.

Terrified of the unknown, I ran helter-skelter. Consequently, I tripped upon a branch, drowning in devious dirt. I was muddy and filthy; I was a scary skeleton, dipped head to toe, in milk chocolate. My heart was racing as I looked at a nearby sign in capital letters, reading: 'BEWARE OF THE FLYING BEES AND VICIOUS ANACONDA SNAKES!!!' Although my legs felt wobbly and unstable, I ran even quicker, not caring if the bees or snakes would pounce upon me.

Minutes later, I spotted an unclear sign and struggled to make heads or tails out of it as there were no arrows or instructions.

Going with my instincts, I just kept running and didn't look back. I hardly knew if the path was taking me to my destination, but I knew stopping was just not an option.

Just then, there was a fading light, flickering in the distance. I walked towards it, shouting for help. I was biting my lip and blinking back another set of tears.

I noticed a vaguely familiar voice. Then, I glanced again and guess who it was? ... Miss Kelly (my Girl Scouts teacher) with the local Search team and Mum and Dad! Relieved, I smiled, then cried then grinned again like the little fool I was. Talk about leaving my class over some butterfly!

"Oh, Daisy Lee! You have done it this time! Come on now, your supper is getting cold!", Mum said as she put her arm around me and we walked to the car.

And as we were about to get into the car, I did see the butterfly again. Only this time, I let it go.

I'm off to bed now but I'll be back tomorrow with another update.

I wonder what adventure awaits me tomorrow.

Love,

Daisy

Lollipops and Rainbows

GENRE: FICTION: POETRY – WRTITING A PRAYER

A Prayer to the Universe

Written by Clare Ford

Dear Universe,

Allow me to see myself now

Allow me to feel strong now

Allow me to know I am enough now

Allow me to follow my guides now

Allow me to feel connected to Source now

Allow the light of love to be my sword now

Allow me to know that I am where I need to be now

Allow me to trust that everything is unfolding as it should now.

Thank you.

SUGGESTED FOLLOW-UP ACTIVITIES

Curious Questions:

1. Why is each line important in this prayer?
2. Why does the prayer thank the Universe at the end?
3. What do the words "allowing" and "gratitude" mean to you?

Aligned Activities:

1. Write a thank you card to an adult you love
2. Think about something you would love to do, and write a diary entry as though you have done it. Use your imagination – it can be absolutely anything at all.
3. Find out about the practise of prayer in different world religions and make a mini fact file.
4. Write a story where your characters are grateful or thankful for something or someone, like Chloe has.

Lollipops and Rainbows

Magic Meditation:

Imagine that you are standing on the very edge of the Universe as your higher self.

Imagine that you can look out and see far and wide, far and wide in every direction.

Imagine that you can see into the past and the future. Take a deep breath in and sit with the knowledge that you have all the answers you need.

On the next in breath say to yourself the mantra:

 "I allow... I allow... I allow....";

And, on the next in breath, say in your head:

"I allow love. I allow light. I allow wisdom. I allow courage."

Sitting with this knowledge, breathe in golden light from Source energy and breathe out white light to the far reaches of the Earth and the Universe.

Then, very slowly, wiggle your fingers and toes and come back to the room.

An Adventure into the Amazon

Written by Chloe Dowsett

Along the extensive, dark green river, floated a cramped, wooden sailing boat bobbing up and down on top of the still water beneath it. Aboard the old, battered boat were two children named Olive and James. Olive had a happy look on her face, smiling with glee as she stared into the deep, gloomy water looking for fish in every colour imaginable. Her long, dark brown hair was tied up in a high ponytail dancing in the soft breeze wearing a jungle-green colour gilet with black trekking trousers and grey boots. James, on the other hand, had an adventurous look on his fair-skinned face, his short, light brown hair wildly blowing everywhere, unlike Olive's, and his navy coat covered in dirty water and dark, wet mud smeared all over his lengthy, grey trousers and brown boots.

The two children sailed along the muddy, green river, leaves getting caught in Olive's luxurious, chocolate-brown hair.

"Look, Olive," shouted James. "The Amazon Rainforest!"

Stood in front of the two curious children, were hundreds of miles of branches and emerald green leaves, a river with crocodiles, dolphins and many more majestic animals.

"WOW!" exclaimed Olive as they both climbed out of the wrecked boat onto the mud, almost falling into the disgusting water. "What should we explore first, James?"

James took a deep breath and with mixed emotions, he looked around himself.

"Let's get back in the boat and sail down the river for a few minutes more," he finally said after thinking for some time. "This is going to be one exciting adventure!"

A few seconds later, both children were inside the boat sailing quickly across the animal-infested river and facing a pitch-black cave. It was camouflaged in leaves and so it looked almost invisible. Olive leapt into the air aiming for the dry land in front of her.

"Argh!" she screamed as she landed on one of her legs, her big, brown eyes were fixed at the strange cave. "That hurt...a lot!"

"Are you OK, Olive?" James asked his sister. He carefully jumped out of the boat to stand next to Olive.

"I'm fine," Olive answered as she grabbed a lengthy stick of bamboo. The two children wandered into the midnight black cave, Olive leaning on the green bamboo, like it was a walking stick. Then, they stepped into the cave.

In a flash, the whole of the Amazon Rainforest transformed into what looked like a fairy-tail jungle!

There were tigers, lions and birds flying in the sky. Every animal you could think of. There was even an incredibly cute koala following Olive and James.

"Oh...my...goodness, James!" Olive stated, astounded at the sight of the now transformed Amazon. "What on earth?!"

"Olive!" immediately shouted James. "There are floating baby pandas holding sticks of bamboo in their paws! Look!"

Olive began walking further and further away from her brother trying to find a panda and looking for other amazing animals lurking in the rainforest too. James also started wandering a long way from Olive and soon enough, the two siblings were half a mile away from each other.

'Oh...no,' thought Olive. "James? James?" she shouted as loud as she could. 'Where could he be?' she wondered. At the thought she might not see her brother again, a small tear rolled down her cheek and she sat on the dusty ground, the koala still near her. Olive shut her sorrowful eyes and sobbed quietly hoping she would find James. James was high up climbing a tree with a smile on his innocent face still trying to find an animal.

"Isn't this fun, Olive?" he called down the tree still thinking his younger sister was there. "Olive? Hello?" and he quickly climbed down to the ground trying to find his sister, but this only made matters worse.

Olive shouted and shouted continuously until her throat was so sore, she couldn't say a word. But this made no difference and they were still lost and far away from anyone. James tried climbing the highest tree near where he was standing and took a long stick from a panda and climbed but still, his beloved sister was nowhere to be found.

At that moment, a large panda flew down to face Olive.

She thought for a few seconds and walked to the panda and settled on an object that was somehow magically hovering behind the panda. Just then, the amazing animal and Olive, feeling quite shocked, floated up into the sky, only slightly below the clouds.

Olive could see thousands of miles of the rainforest, including her brother!

The intelligent panda immediately flew down to James as if it knew just what Olive wanted it to do.

At last, the two children were reunited with each other once again! Olive and James both hugged and set off to find the river.

The two sailed home with an immense number of memories in their heads and feeling enormously happy and thankful for each other.

Diary Entry: The Journey

Written by Clare Ford

29th April 3017

"5, 4, 3, 2, 1 BLAST OFF!!!!"

And we were off! Up and away! This is the day that I had been waiting for... and now it arrived! My very first time in a space rocket. Obviously, some of my friends' parents had already been up in one – but now was my opportunity, as winner of a poetry competition. Yay!!!!

The purpose of the trip was to find this new tiny planet and to decide how we were going to populate it. After our voyage of discovery, a huge committee meeting will be held with the wise elders, luminaries, leaders, teachers, healers and children to design how we would like the planet to be. But that's a story for another day.

Up, up, up we zoomed, through the Earth's atmosphere and into the inky blue of space.

Through the port holes I began to distinguish stars twinkling in the distant inky blackness; on the other side were the planets of my ancestors Andromeda and Pleiades, surrounded by a beautiful blue and green swirling star dust.

We travelled on and on... further and further, until we reached the very edge of the Universe itself.

As the spaceship cruised along, its engines barely purring, we were able to hear the Universe's own song through special speakers.

We could hear the planetary dance and the orchestral notes of galaxies, punctuated by melodic light from stars and moonbeams. We could hear deep melodies from Jupiter and Saturn drifting out to us in the furthest reaches of the Universe.

It was the purest, deepest combination of sounds and vibrations I had ever heard. It was, simply, beautifully majestic.

SUGGESTED FOLLOW-UP ACTIVITIES

Curious Questions:

1. How would you feel if you won a rocket trip by entering a poetry competition?

2. What would be the most important thing you would want people to do on your planet? Why?

Aligned Actions:

1. Write a descriptive narrative about your new planet, like Yousif has. Include some of the ideas below to help you.
    a. Who lives on the new planet?
    b. What are they doing there?
    c. How do they feel?
    d. What is the planet like? What is on it?
    e. What is the weather like?
    f. How many moons and suns are there?

2. Write your own version of the diary entry as a comic strip, like Devlin and Daniil have.

3. Compose your own Universal music – use as many instruments as you like, or even make some of your own.

4. Listen to some music and paint whatever is conjured up in your mind. It doesn't have to be a particular picture/image – it can be shapes or marks of any shape, size or colour.

5. Write a short journalistic or newspaper report about what the travellers discover.

6. Create a tourist guide to persuade people to join you on your newly discovered planet.

7. Write a balanced argument about why human beings should or should not populate a different planet. Be sure to use: PEE (point, evidence, explain).

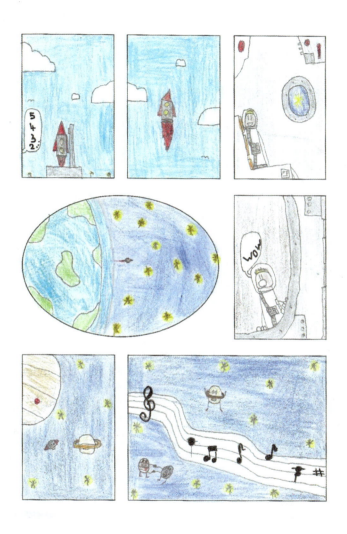

The Journey Comic Strip by Devlin Clayton

Magic Meditation:

Imagine floating out in space at the edge of the Universe.

Imagine being weightless.

Breathe into this feeling of not being tied down by anything.

Allow yourself to feel free and happy.

Nothing can harm you here.

You are limitless.

You are without limits.

Imagine you are one of the stars taking part in the cosmic dance.

Breathe into this feeling of being alive.

Breathe into this Universal energy.

Breathe it into every cell of your body.

You are a light being.

You are made of starlight.

Then, very slowly, wiggle your fingers and toes and come back to the room.

The World of Pandora

Written and Illustrated by Yousif Mahmood

One sizzling sunny day, the clock above the door was ticking quietly and lightly, it was 5:50. Max looked at it and was shocked. He noticed that it was school as always and the bus was about to leave in 10 minutes, so he RAPIDLY got off his big blue bunk bed, put his clean clothes on, brushed his hair then he dashed outside like lightning from his homey home. He arrived at BSB and noticed his friends in the playground playing a game called 'Lava Guy'.

"Tag, you're it!" giggled Jack, catching Thomas.

 "Pause, it didn't count," complained Thomas crossing his arms.

"Just stop arguing and catch us since you're it," added Ben and Sam together exhaustedly.

Meanwhile, Miss Clare entered the playground with three kids who were begging her to allow them to ring the bell. Instead, she rang the bell.

The students flooded the corridor ready to begin their learning.

Max and his classmates ran to their seats and took out their whiteboards and markers. Max strolled to his tray to fetch his whiteboard and whiteboard marker but then, he realized that his whiteboard marker was out of ink.

Max was escorted to Miss Honeybee and requested her to give him a new whiteboard marker, so off they went.

Meanwhile, the children continued chatting while Max was looking around the classroom. Surprisingly, he found an odd, strange statue of a horse. Max kept on staring at it. Then he thought of stealing it, but the dilemma was that the statue was not his property. He had a little while to think about it until he chose the wrong option...

And you guessed it...

He did take it.

SUDDENLY, MAX ENDED UP IN AN OUTLANDISH PLANET!

He was teleported to AN ULTRA SATISFYING PLACE CALLED PANDORA. He closed his eyes and couldn't focus on anything else except escaping from the uninhabitable place for humans. Max was really anxious, lost and couldn't believe his eyes. Pandora was so vivid like a crystal-clear world. The sky was as charming as a lilac flower; it was changing from a mystifying blend of lavender, maroon and navy blue. The ground and trees were glowing gently as he moved. As Max was walking, he could smell the Pleasant Pure Petrichor. He felt the foggy air as if he were a moist frog or toad. The trees were 100 times taller than the trees on Earth.

The gigantic gas planet, which is the size of Saturn, looked very impressive!

MAX
    WAS
        LOST!

He had to find a shelter and fast! He sprinted, flummoxed, until he found a cozy, warm straw hut. He was delighted to find a shelter and he fell into a deep unconscious sleep!

The next offensive murky morning, he wasn't in the hut. He somehow ended up next to a nearby towering turquoise tree. It was all silent when he carefully looked around, but the hut was not nearby at all.

Suddenly, something grabbed his attention! For a moment, Max's heart began to race in a rush of dread. Some royal blue humanoid creatures (10 times taller than the tallest person on Earth) called Na'vis were surrounding him ready to battle him. He was never ready to battle so checked if there was survival stuff in his Solar System Styled Schoolbag. He rapidly unzipped the bag, then he found out that his books and stationery equipment had turned into some sticks!?!

An insane, odd monster appeared and fiercely attacked the royal blue Na'vis as they started to tremble with fear. It was twelve times taller than Max, whose heart pumped as quickly as the Direhorse's. He had no chance to run away so he just threw the sticks as far as he could.

The Direhorse acted like a domestic animal. It picked up the sticks with its mouth and gave them back to Max, sticking its tongue out.

Max happily wondered if the Direhorse could become his Pandorian Friend! (Max and Dune the Direhorse).

Afterwards, the statue of Dune the Direhorse reappeared! It was glowing as if there were a message. Max noticed that the horse of the statue was Dune the Direhorse!

"What if I touch the statue?" he asked himself.

"Will I teleport back to class?" he asked Dune. Thirty seconds later, Dune the Direhorse pointed at the statue with its hoof, as a message for Max to touch the statue. Max listened to Dune as his Pandorian Friend. Max looked at Dune the Direhorse and said a Good- Bye.

For a moment, Max realised that if he touched it, he would teleport back to our beautiful beloved Earth.

Max was peacefully enchanted.

Thankfully, he picked it up and immediately teleported back to his class, feeling extraordinary and completely delightful.

Somehow, even though Max had travelled to another planet and back, he did not have a speck of dirt or evidence of Pandora on him.

"Max, Max, Max?" repeated Miss Honeybee continuously, checking the science notebooks.

"Yes, Miss Honeybee, yes!" he replied confused, staring at his friends and teachers from the back of the classroom, realizing that he did not have the Direhorse Statue.

"Did you hear that scientists discovered a brand-new planet? Apparently, there are animals and everything! Wouldn't it be so cool to visit?" his teacher asked, waiting for an answer.

Max smiled, trying to decide whether or not to share his adventure with the class; furthermore he did not think that they would believe his adventure and Dune the Direhorse, so he kept it as a secret.

The Magic Big Mac

Written by Daniil Domnych

Once upon a time, there lived a loving family who loved to go to one of the most popular junk food restaurants called McDonald`s. They went to McDonald`s twice a week, so this means they were quite fat. In the family there were two children: a boy called George and a girl called Bailey. The parents were called Katie and Sam.

They were going to McDonald`s for their dinner, so they took the closest bus to High Street. They just entered the restaurant when suddenly music started playing and there was confetti everywhere as a weird looking old lady came over to them with the biggest burger the family have ever seen!

The old lady looked at the whole family and said to George "Take this amazing burger that we made for you; once you eat it you will have three wishes and you can wish whatever you like!"

So George decided to try the burger but as soon as he took a bite...

The world was spinning and George thought "This is the end of my life!" (but he didn't really believe it was).

When the spinning stopped and George sat up to find himself on the ground which looked red. He saw that there was something looming over him - a huge ugly bird, but it was actually a giant lion pig.

"Come with me and we will try to return you back to your own planet Earth" it said to George. But George didn't go because he couldn't stop wondering about what his family were thinking while he was gone. Are they happy? Are they mad at the old lady?

George remembered that he had three wishes so he wanted to try and see if it was true or not. He said "I wish I had a trillion pounds!" Nothing happened.

Out of thin air, a huge bag with a zip on it appeared. When George opened it he found the biggest amount of money he has ever seen in real life, so he asked the lion pig "What do you wish for?" (George also named the lion pig Trackula).

Trackula answered "I would love to be on your planet for the rest of my life!" George then did something he never thought would happen - he grabbed Trackula and quickly said, "I wish we were both on planet Earth.".

Suddenly both George and Trackula were on Planet Earth, next to George's family who all screamed in terror when they saw Trackula - but when they saw George they sighed with relief and asked George where he had been.

"Long story short I had an amazing adventure," he explained. They all hugged each other and went home but when they did they found whirling vortex of sand in the middle of the living room. They all looked at each other and decided to go in...

Guided Rainbow Meditation

Close your eyes and come on a journey with me. We are going on a special adventure together to help you find something amazing. Are you ready?

Take a deep breath in. Sit with your feet firmly planted on the floor and your back up straight. Be aware of each breath, filling your stomach, filling your lungs and filling your chest. Allow your breathing to slow down. Become fully present, feeling yourself connected to your chair; feeling the air on the hairs on your arms; feeling the ground hard beneath your feet. We will soon come back to this place on our return.

Imagine you are following me up a colourful spiral staircase made of glass which is in the middle of nature... We are on the bottom step, which is a beautiful, vibrant red. Allow yourself to sit on this step for a while, looking about you and inhaling the red colour. Fill your whole body with this colour, right down to the tips of your fingers and the tips of your toes.

Next, we are moving up to the orange step. This is a beautiful sparkly golden orange which shimmers when you stand on it. Again, let's sit here a while and look about. Take a deep breath in as you look at the golden sun shimmering through the treetops. Fill your whole body with this colour and notice with curiosity where this colour is reflected in nature. Feel the warmth spread through your entire body as if fills with sparkling golden orange light.

Now we are moving on to a yellow step. This is a sparkly, pale yellow. Fill your whole body with this colour as you take a deep breath in as you look at the pale, yellow sun shimmering through the treetops... feel your body tingling as it fills up with this beautiful light.

We're stepping up now to the green step. This is a beautiful magical green which reflects all the shades and hues from nature. Take a deep breath in as you look at the shimmering leaves and swaying grass. Fill your whole body with this colour and notice with curiosity where this colour is reflected in nature.

When you are ready, we are going to take the next step up to the pale blue step. This is a calming, relaxing blue which shimmers when you stand on it. Take a deep breath in as you look at the huge expanse of blue sky above you. Fill your whole body with this colour and notice with curiosity how it makes you feel.

Now we are moving onto the indigo step.

Now we are standing on a clear white step

Next, we are moving up to a silver step

Now you are in the Angelic realm on a golden step.

The Return of Fruit Island

Written and Illustrated by Malak Mahmood

Once upon a time, on fantastic Fruit Island, there ruled a wise king named King Pineapple and a majestic queen called Queen Sugar Plum. On Fruit Island, there were well-planted flavourful fruits and the sky was as sapphire and as smooth as the sea. The green grass was as soft as fur. You could hear the birds chirping their musical melodies.

All the people liked the queen and king because they were kindhearted and fair. But the only hopelessness in the queen's life was that she was desperate for a child but did not get one as she wanted, and it grieved her sorely. One day, the king got a marvellous idea and joyfully explained it to the queen, "Since tomorrow is your blessed birthday, I am going to invite a wizard who supports others to make their dreams come true!" The queen was amazed by the idea.

One day passed by, and it was the queen's birthday,

in the castle, there was a hilarious comedian, a famous and well-educated scientist and many more important people but most important of all, the wonderful wizard. At the end of the party, the wizard, king and queen were together in the wide hall room. Once there, the wizard chanted a magical spell: *"Hokus-Pokus-O-Bring-The-Queen-Whatever-She-Dreams-Of!"* and he gave the queen a bottle that contained a pink liquid.

The queen drank the liquid slowly but, suddenly the wizard turned into an evil wizard and evilly explained, "I am Agent Orange and, once the baby is 10, I will rule this fascinating Island, and no one will stop me. Hahaha!!!" and he disappeared into thin air.

The king and queen were petrified and hoped he had not done damage to the child. A few months later she gave birth to a baby! They decided to call the baby Ela.

Ten years passed and the king and queen never told Ela about what happened before she was with them. At midnight everything changed. The royal family was teleported to a straw hut whilst Agent Orange was sitting on the golden throne laughing his evil laugh. Ela was confused about what was happening and started to ask her parents questions like "What just happened?" and "Why are we here?"

The king and queen were nervous and told her what happened. She was shocked by what she heard and stated "Well... we won't give up! We need to think of something to stop this madman!"

The family happily agreed and started to think of a plan. The queen's face lit up as she settled on an idea.

"How about we spread out and find something useful to help us?" she suggested

Next morning, the family dashed out of the hut to find help, but no luck could be found, so they decided to try again the next day.

When Ela woke up, she went out to play on top of a hill near their small hut, where she found a gloomy cave. She wished to explore the cave, so Ela took a deep breath and went in. Unexpectedly, she found a sad fairy trapped in a cage, so Ela swiftly called for her mum and dad to help the fairy.

 "I thank you with all my heart, what can I do to help you in return?" thanked Fairy Flora.

"The wizard that we invited to the queen's birthday was an evil agent called Agent Orange who has teleported us into a small cottage, and stolen our castle." explained Ela.

"We need your help!" said the king sadly. Luckily, the fairy knew how to undo the spell. The fairy understood and replied,

 "Ohhh, now I know! So, let me think of a plan... here it is, I will make an enchanted potion and you will creep with it to the kitchen to add it in Agent Orange's favourite tomato soup. Then, wait and see the magic!"

That was an astonishing idea so, they did as they were told.

At midnight, they dressed up as chefs and when they met the guards they let them in because they hated Agent Orange as he was unfair and rude to the people. So, they rapidly added the marvellous potion and when Agent Orange guzzled up the enjoyable soup, he teleported to Mushroom Land which is dreadfully stinky!

The royal family were soon on their throne again and the fairy received an amazing prize for helping.

"Thank you for your wonderful help, we appreciate it," thanked Princess Ela.

"I was just helping and getting our incredible rulers back!" responded Flora.

The family lived together forever in peace and joy.

Grassy Meadows and the Mystery of the Puppy Park

Written and Illustrated by Mia Waterworth

It all started on a sunny Summer day.

It was a warm afternoon and there was a smell of freshly cut grass in the air. However, this was no ordinary day. Grassy Meadows puppy playground is usually bustling with dogs and lots of activity but today it was deserted.

It was eerily quiet, and no sound could be heard not even the birds tweeting. That was except, the panting of Hiccup the fluffy clumsy sheep dog. Why was Hiccup there alone?

Where was everyone else?

On the other side town, Holly and Boz were wagging their tails as they were heading towards their favourite park to see their friend Hiccup.

Nothing could spoil their happiness as Grassy
Meadows is the ultimate theme park for dogs.
They were always to excited play there.

Holly and Boz were best friends who have known
each other since they were puppies. Boz was
a mature yet boisterous and energetic mutt who was
the leader of the pack. As with dogs his age he was
very wise. His chocolate wiry fur and loveable eyes
always attracted the attention of children wherever
he went. You can hear the sound of
"Ah Adorable'" when the children walked by and
petted him.

Holly adored him. She was an intelligent and
loyal watch dog who carefully protected her owners
and friends. She was always aware of
her surroundings and on the lookout for any
danger. Even Holly felt uneasy about how still
the Grassy Meadows was today. Her honey coat of soft
fur stood on end.

What was going on?

Holly and Boz arrived at the park. In the distance
was a faint outline of Hiccup. The clumsy sheepdog
looked up and ran towards them. She fell, then
ran, then fell again, you get the idea until she heard ...
"HICCUP!!!'" Holly and Boz chorused together.

After they sniffed hello, they talked about the rumour
of a new pet shop opening in town.

Suddenly, they heard a rumbling and felt
the ground shake below their feet. Boz
nervously gazed up.

Lollipops and Rainbows

'Look at the trees' he barked.

They all looked up at the shaking trees. Holly the watch dog growled and howled as a warning to others to run.

What was happening?

Darkness fell across the park and they felt sudden a chill in the air. They knew it was time to go home. Their hearts were beating fast as they ran back.

Then Boz broke their nervous silence.
"Shall we go back tonight at quarter to Midnight?" Boz barked.

Little did he know what they would find…

As quarter to midnight drew nearer Boz was regretting what he had said to the others. Holly lifted her sleepy head from the bed and looked at the clock.

She whispered, "It's time."

They made sure their owners were tucked up asleep in bed, then crept out of the backdoor and through the creaky loose panel in the fence. They joined their neighbour Hiccup on the other side.

Nervously, Holly and Boz ran to the park with Hiccup who stumbled as usual to keep up with them every once in a while.

They all stopped dead in their tracks.

They were unable to move any further. Something had blocked their path.

"OH NO!!!" said Boz.

"AHW AHW!" yelped Hiccup.

"Woof!!!" Holly barked angrily.

They were faced with a huge digger towering over them like a monster. The park had heavy metal chains around the fence imprisoning their grassy meadows and all that lived in there. That's why the park was deserted this morning .Everyone knew they would be trapped in there and not able to escape .

They had to get help and soon!

They ran back home worried. They had faced their worst nightmare that the playground would be demolished.

The following morning, they informed every dog in the village about what was happening to the puppy park. They agreed to meet back at the park that afternoon to discuss what they could do about this.

Later that day, the dogs arrived at Grass Meadows and to their astonishment, they found...

An extended Puppy Park with a fabulous dog zipline and the newly built Pet shop that sold treats.

"THE NEW AND IMPROVED PUPPY PARK!!!" Holly, Boz and Hiccup barked together in relief.

Meet the Authors & Illustrators

Lollipops and Rainbows

Oskar Ford

AGE 16

COUNTRY England

INTERESTS/HOBBIES Reading historical novels

ONE INTERESTING FACT
I love cats!

WHAT I LIKED ABOUT BEING PART OF THIS PROJECT
Helping my Mum!

Lillian Strickland

AGE 14

COUNTRY England

INTERESTS/HOBBIES:
Singing, drama, history

ONE INTERESTING FACT:
I have a dog named Figgy Pudding.

WHAT I LIKED ABOUT BEING PART OF THIS PROJECT:
It was satisfying to draw.

Lucy Chandler

AGE: 9 and 3 quarters

COUNTRY: England

INTERESTS/HOBBIES:
Reading, drawing, listening to music and climbing

ONE INTERESTING FACT:
I appeared on TV when I was a few months old

WHAT I LIKED ABOUT BEING PART OF THIS PROJECT:
Being able to write a really good book!

Lollipops and Rainbows

Scarlet Hodder

AGE: 8

COUNTRY: England

INTERESTS/HOBBIES:
Drama, singing

ONE INTERESTING FACT:
I have a dog named Bonnie.

WHAT I LIKED ABOUT BEING PART OF THIS PROJECT:
Imagining the story and doing my own illustrations.

Ellie Clements

AGE 9

COUNTRY England

INTERESTS/HOBBIES:
I like skateboarding and painting.

ONE INTERESTING FACT:
I love mystical creatures!

WHAT I LIKED ABOUT BEING PART OF THIS PROJECT:
I liked planning my story.

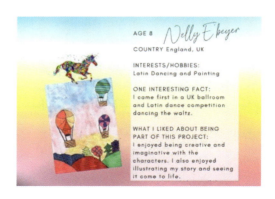

Nelly Ebeyer

AGE 8

COUNTRY England, UK

INTERESTS/HOBBIES:
Latin Dancing and Painting

ONE INTERESTING FACT:
I came first in a UK ballroom and Latin dance competition dancing the waltz.

WHAT I LIKED ABOUT BEING PART OF THIS PROJECT:
I enjoyed being creative and imaginative with the characters. I also enjoyed illustrating my story and seeing it come to life.

Lollipops and Rainbows

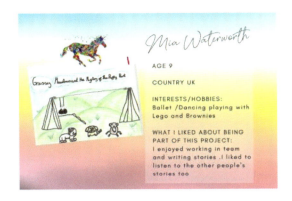

Mia Waterworth

AGE 9

COUNTRY UK

INTERESTS/HOBBIES:
Ballet /Dancing playing with Lego and Brownies

WHAT I LIKED ABOUT BEING PART OF THIS PROJECT:
I enjoyed working in team and writing stories .I liked to listen to the other people's stories too

Devlin O'Brien

AGE 9

COUNTRY Ireland

INTERESTS/HOBBIES: Creating comics; reading and anything to do with Star Wars

ONE INTERESTING FACT:
My family adopted a dog called Lexie from a rescue this summer. I love her!

WHAT I LIKED ABOUT BEING PART OF THIS PROJECT:
I am really grateful to have been allowed to contribute to the project. I liked the challenge a lot and it was fun because it wasn't like school work :)

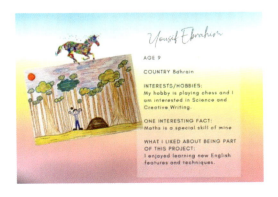

Yousif Ebrahim

AGE 9

COUNTRY Bahrain

INTERESTS/HOBBIES:
My hobby is playing chess and I am interested in Science and Creative Writing.

ONE INTERESTING FACT:
Maths is a special skill of mine

WHAT I LIKED ABOUT BEING PART OF THIS PROJECT:
I enjoyed learning new English features and techniques.

Lollipops and Rainbows

Malak Ebrahim

AGE 9

COUNTRY Bahrain

INTERESTS/HOBBIES:
Space, Art and Creative Writing

ONE INTERESTING FACT:
I am very curious and I love learning new things

WHAT I LIKED ABOUT BEING PART OF THIS PROJECT:
I enjoyed imagining my story step by step.

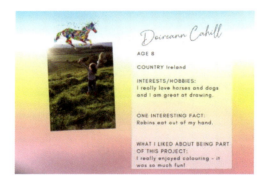

Doireann Cahill

AGE 8

COUNTRY Ireland

INTERESTS/HOBBIES:
I really love horses and dogs and I am great at drawing.

ONE INTERESTING FACT:
Robins eat out of my hand.

WHAT I LIKED ABOUT BEING PART OF THIS PROJECT:
I really enjoyed colouring - it was so much fun!

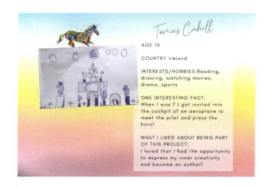

Tomas Cahill

AGE 10

COUNTRY Ireland

INTERESTS/HOBBIES: Reading, drawing, watching movies, drama, sports

ONE INTERESTING FACT:
When I was 7 I got invited into the cockpit of an aeroplane to meet the pilot and press the horn!

WHAT I LIKED ABOUT BEING PART OF THIS PROJECT:
I loved that I had the opportunity to express my inner creativity and become an author!

Lollipops and Rainbows

Emilia Catanach
AGE 8
COUNTRY England, UK
INTERESTS/HOBBIES: Sloths, Reading, Singing, Writing
ONE INTERESTING FACT: My best friend is called Jasmine, the name of a flower.
WHAT I LIKED ABOUT BEING PART OF THIS PROJECT: I liked being creative and I liked my mum helping me when I got stuck.

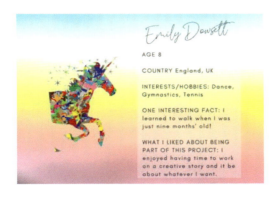

Emily Dowsett
AGE 8
COUNTRY England, UK
INTERESTS/HOBBIES: Dance, Gymnastics, Tennis
ONE INTERESTING FACT: I learned to walk when I was just nine months' old!
WHAT I LIKED ABOUT BEING PART OF THIS PROJECT: I enjoyed having time to work on a creative story and it about whatever I want.

Chloe Dowsett
AGE 10
COUNTRY England, UK
INTERESTS/HOBBIES: Art, Drawing, Singing, Dancing
ONE INTERESTING FACT: I did a violin solo performance to 150 people when I was 9.
WHAT I LIKED ABOUT BEING PART OF THIS PROJECT: Learning about what makes a great story and how to write one.

TEACHING NOTES

Please refer to the elements I have included for each style of writing to help you pinpoint exactly what it is you are looking for to support your students' success.

You can find a complimentary teaching session for each writing style in the Switched ON! Academy.

Lollipops and Rainbows

Artemis' Birthday
Creative Writing
Myth/Legend

What we are looking for:

Clear paragraphs	✓
Beginning, Middle, End	✓
Varied sentence structure	✓
High level vocabulary	✓
High level punctuation	✓
Correct grammar eg: with dialogue	✓
Characterisation	✓
Plot	✓
Interesting and engaging	✓

powerful opening sentence to hook the reader and instill curiosity to read on...

Artemis was no ordinary girl, and so her birthday was going to be like no other.

typical start for a fairy story, using description of setting and characters to set the scene.

Long, long, ago deep in the forgotten mists of time, the faint hooting of an owl was carried on a soft breeze to an ancient woodland grove, where Artemis was resting in her favourite place, against the gnarled fallen log of a great oak tree. Artemis was waiting for her father, who was meeting her to give her a present for her tenth birthday.

clearly differentiated paragraphs to show time passing.

Needless to say, she could barely contain her excitement and waiting seemed like an eternity. "Practise patience my dear," she could almost hear her grandmother whispering to her.

planting clues for the reader about other characters; values etc.

So, with a deep breath, she sat up straight, with her feet firmly planted on the ground, and raised her face to the sunlight that was streaming through the treetops.

Within seconds, Artemis could feel her breathing slowing,

Lollipops and Rainbows

Sentence starting with adverb	<u>Suddenly</u>, she heard the rustle of leaves, and drumming of hooves. Then silence. She felt something behind her. She stopped breathing.
Sentence starting with adjective	<u>Silhouetted</u> in the flickering light was a giant shadow – of a bear, but not the brown bear she was used to seeing in these woods.
Sentence starting with subject	<u>Her father</u> was taking too long. The shadows spread and lengthened through the trees, throwing dappled patterns onto the forest floor. Anxiously, she estimated the time again.
Rhetorical question	<u>Could it be him?</u>
Short phrase for effect and to build	<u>Coming closer.</u>
Ellipsis	<u>Something felt strange</u>…
Time connective	<u>As time went on</u>, other creatures appeared too, such as the wolf, eagle and bear. Artemis was unafraid and sat quietly and still so that she could fully appreciate the gifts that each animal
compound sentence linking with "and"	his huge body and warm cloak, wrapped protectively in his strong arm. <u>She looked into his strong, kind face and saw the deep wisdom in his clear eyes.</u>
use of dash - high level punctuation	She knew instinctively that this would be a gift like no other – for her father was Zeus, God of the Gods.
Start with subordinate clause	Carefully unwrapping the moss and leaves from the bundle that her father had given her, Artemis discovered she was
Repetition for effect and to emphasise importance	holding <u>a wooden box</u>. <u>A wooden box</u> that was similar to the one at home that her grandmother kept her special rings in. <u>A wooden box</u> that felt ancient and very, very special.
complex sentence with subordinate clause	<u>Artemis carefully traced the engravings etched on the curved lid with her index finger, trying to fathom the symbols that she found there.</u>
Correct use of dialogue; new speaker, new line.	"What is in this box papa?" she thought breathlessly…
	"This is the box of the ancients," he explained, "It has been handed down to specially chosen people, who are the guardians and light workers of the Earth. And now, my daughter Artemis, I am handing this box to you. In it are the answers to all questions – asked and as yet unasked. In it is the wisdom of the ancients from the beginning of Dawn."

When Spirit Wolf Lost Her Spirit
Creative Writing
Myth/Legend

What we are looking for:

Clear paragraphs	✓
Beginning, Middle, End	✓
Varied sentence structure	✓
High level vocabulary	✓
High level punctuation	✓
Correct grammar eg: with dialogue	✓
Characterisation	✓
Plot	✓
Interesting and engaging	✓

powerful opening sentence to hook the reader and set the scene

Never in history had such an event occurred. In the centre of a leafy glade, Spirit Wolf was lying, still and exhausted.

introduce mythical creatures and use descriptive writing. Introduce the dilemma or problem.

Moon Wolf howled, long and low, to summon Mother Nature to help. The wind rustled the leaves in the glade, and woodland creatures crept out to surround Spirit Wolf. "What shall we do?" they wondered...

"Is Spirit Wolf ill? What has happened? Has Spirit Wolf lost her spirit?" Fire Wolf stood up amongst the pack and suggested that they make a medicine wheel from twigs and leaves. This wheel points to the four corners of the earth and to the heavens above and the earth below.

Since the dawn of time it has been used to summon wisdom

Lollipops and Rainbows

"We need to get Spirit Wolf to the Worry Tree," she explained gravely. "Something is troubling her heart and soul and the Worry Tree will listen and take the worries away. Then Spirit Wolf can heal and will feel strengthened." So with that, the pack of wolves and the woodland creatures made a bed of straw and moss which they used to carry Spirit Wolf carefully over the rocky terrain to the lonely Worry Tree on the edge of the plain. They laid her down with care.

They stood in a respective circle around her and sent beautiful pink sparkling healing energy from their hearts to each other, to Spirit Wolf and to all of the Earth.

Quietly, Howling Wolf started a slow humming, and the other wolves gently joined in until the wheel of medicine lifted itself up from the barren soil and span above Spirit Wolf's body, this way and that, swirling and whirling until all that could be seen was a myriad of colours.

A bright translucent rainbow surrounded Spirit Wolf's body and a beautiful white glow lit up the area under the Worry

the sky above and emitted a long, beautiful eerie howl which reverberated around the earth, to all dimensions, to all galaxies and stars in the Universe.

"My journey has brought me home. I have found what I was searching for. It is within me.

I have everything I need inside of me, in my heart and in my soul. I thought my spirit was shattered into hundreds of little tiny pieces, but now I feel whole again. Thank you."

The wolves and creatures cheered and went back to the glade, rejoicing that Spirit Wolf felt whole again.

How the Earth was Made
Creation Poem
Fiction/Rhyme

What we are looking for:

Syllabic pattern	✓
Rhyming pattern	✓
Poetry technique: alliteration	✓
Poetry technique: repetition	✓
Poetry technique: personification	✓
Poetry technique: onomatopoeia	✓
Meaningful	✓
High level vocabulary	✓
Interesting and engaging	✓

Lollipops and Rainbows

syllabic pattern: 8,8,6,6, repeated in each stanza

rhyming pattern A,B,C,B repeated in each stanza

A star dropped into the ocean,

A moonbeam fell out of the sky,

Stardust mixed with sunlight,

A tear began to dry.

powerful imagery

high level vocab

personification

near rhyme

A soft rainbow made a light bridge,

A cloud transmitted a kind thought,

Lightning mixed with thunder,

The clouds began to part.

high level vocab

alliteration

onomatopoeia

Sunlight cascaded through blackness,

Deep golden light felt soft, damp ground,

Silver drops covered vast seas,

Yellow sparks shone around.

Lollipops and Rainbows

A Recipe for Sunshine
Instructional Writing

What we are looking for:

Chronological sequence	✓
Fronted adverbials	✓
Imperative verbs	✓
Clear, precise language	✓
A result	✓

You will need: ⟵——————

BEFORE you write your recipe, make a note of all the equipment your reader will need, and set it out in a list with bullet points or numbers, and illustrations or diagrams if you wish.

I have had fun with writing this quirky recipe by using alliteration for effect, but this is not necessary for your recipe to be effective.

- A sprinkle of smiles
- A pint of peace
- A cup of kisses
- A handful of healing
- A touch of tickles
- A colander of cuddles
- A kilo of kindness
- A litre of laughter
- A spoonful of stardust
- A helping hand
- A whole lot of love
- A bowl
- A mixing spoon

Lollipops and Rainbows

Use "bossy" imperative verbs so your reader knows exactly what to do.

Instructions:

Number your instructions.

Use time connectives and fronted adverbials to start each sentence, ensuring they are in chronological order.

1. First, take your bowl and a mixing spoon.

2. Next, add the peace, cuddles and kindness, and fold until soft.

3. Then, add the kisses and laughter, with a helping hand and love.

4. Finally, sprinkle smiles, tickles and stardust

Lollipops and Rainbows

The Swan' Song
Story Writing Based on a Traditional Tale

What we are looking for:

Clear paragraphs	✓
Beginning, Middle, End	✓
Varied sentence structure	✓
High level vocabulary	✓
High level punctuation	✓
Correct grammar eg: with dialogue	✓
Characterisation	✓
Plot	✓
Interesting and engaging	✓

Lollipops and Rainbows

Strong opening sentence clearly stating what the story is about.

This is a story about a swan.... Or should I say a rather strange grey fluffy looking bird who didn't fit in anywhere.

Chatty tone to engage the reader, easy and comfortable from the first paragraph.

As you probably know, the little cygnet was looked after by a mother duck and its brothers and sisters were the baby ducklings in the family. Needless to say, the cygnet could neither move nor swim with the same grace and ease as the ducklings, and began to feel very out of place. It was much larger than its yellow, fluffy siblings and was very clumsy. The ducklings began to tease the cygnet, out of ear shot of their mother, of course – and the cygnet felt lonely and sad and different.

Descriptive setting to begin the story itself.

One early morning, our grey fluffy friend set off, head down, to live elsewhere. Passing a near-by farm, the cygnet approached the resident sheep dog, to make a new friend. But it barked loudly and bared its canine teeth and the cygnet was afraid... As it turned to run, the farmyard geese gave chase too

Paragraphs easily differentiated, starting in a variety of different ways to keep the writing interesting

Eventually, stopping at a small pond to drink, the cygnet noticed a large tear plop into the water. It looked closer and after a brief minute of surprise <u>realised</u> it belonged to him... The reason the cygnet was surprised was because it no longer resembled the grey, fluffy ungainly animal from a few weeks earlier.

use of ellipsis

high level vocabulary to add interest and imagery

<u>The cygnet</u> had turned into a beautiful swan at <u>last...</u> And, as it <u>gazed disbelievingly</u> into the pond, the swan saw a flock of white birds <u>reflected</u> in the sky above. "<u>Wow!</u> It thought to itself – those birds look so <u>gracious</u>... They are flying with such ease and they are so white – they look <u>majestic</u> against the blue sky."

correct use of dialogue

<u>Unbelievably,</u> the flock of swans were flying towards the pond, and landed gracefully nearby. One of the swans approached our friend and said, "We have been looking everywhere for you. It's time for you to come and fly away with us. We are your family." As the swan felt another large tear roll down its white cheek, it let out a sigh of relief.

"<u>Well,</u> what are you waiting for?" asked the main swan. "You can fly; you can swim. Let us show you the beautiful lake where we live."

Lollipops and Rainbows

A Song for Humanity

Song/Lyrics
Poetry/Rhyme

What we are looking for:

Syllabic pattern	✓
Rhyming pattern	✓
Poetry technique: rhyme and near rhyme	✓
Poetry technique: repetition	✓
Poetry technique: imagery	✓
Meaningful	✓
High level vocabulary	✓
Interesting and engaging	✓

Lollipops and Rainbows

CHORUS or REFRAIN repeated after each verse or "stanza"

Gaia Earth, Gaia Earth, mother and nurturer
Father Sky, Father Sky, guide and protector

Syllabic pattern repeated in each stanza: 10, 10, 10, 10

Open up my heart; surrender to love,
Open up my voice and hear my heart sing,
Open up my eyes and see my true self,
Open my heart for the light to flood in.

Repetition, rhyme and near rhyme for effect

Gaia Earth, Gaia Earth, mother and nurturer
Father Sky, Father Sky, guide and protector

Using the senses as a theme in this stanza

See our Universe gently pulsating,
Hear sweet birdsong and gentle rain falling,
Sense my star fam'ly sparkling and twinkling,
Taste hot winds shifting, cool waters soothing.

Using apostrophe for contraction to maintain syllabic pattern

Gaia Earth, Gaia Earth, mother and nurturer
Father Sky, Father Sky, guide and protector

Beautiful light of the Ancients to guide us,
Wisdom and courage available to us,
Feelings of peace and contentment inside us,
The whole world in harm'ny, singing with us.

Who Am I?

Writing a Speech
Non-Fiction

What we are looking for:

Clear paragraphs	✓
Beginning, Middle, End	✓
Varied sentence structure	✓
High level vocabulary	✓
High level punctuation	✓
Correct grammar	✓
Technique: rhetorical question	✓
Technique: rule of three	✓
Interesting and engaging	✓

WHO AM I?
Written by Clare Ford

Greeting and rhetorical question to engage the audience.

Hello and good day. Who is this person that you see sitting in front of you today?

Delivering new info to capture attention

Well, I'll start with my name, Clare, which means light and bright and clear, derived from the Latin term "Clarus", and the Medieval name Clara. You'll have to decide if my name fits!

Loop back to title of speech

Who am I? Let's start off with definitions to do with relationships...

Use rhetorical question to ensure listener is still engaged.

I am a mother of two teenage boys, a daughter, a sister, an aunty, a step-grandmother, an ex-wife and a partner... A survivor of depression and anxiety.

Does that really help you get a sense of Who I AM? Or actually are these just labels? So often we define ourselves by the people who are in our lives. The people and the circumstances that happen to us aren't necessarily the definition that we need to have. We are more than our circumstances!

Surprise listener with unusual approach in information

A Piscean with rising Leo, Numerology Life Path 7; Pleiadean Indigo Starseed....

No – it doesn't necessarily mean a lot to everybody, although these are still definitions that some people find extremely important and interesting and take very seriously indeed. But actually these are also just labels so we need to peel away that layer of the onion too...

Let's delve a bit deeper now. Who Am I?

Getting into the main part of the speech with questions, rule of three and personal anecdotes.

I am a compassionate, caring, intelligent person who likes to help people reach their full potential. This is why I have been a teacher for 15 years; I am now a private tutor and a qualified transformational life coach and energy healer.

Is that getting closer to the essence of who I am? Well, it tells us about what I do and why I do it... But actually lots of people may be like that. So what is it that makes us uniquely who we are? What is it that makes me uniquely different from other caring, compassionate, intelligent, wonderful life coaches, healers and teachers?

I have, in my life, undergone some very difficult situations and circumstances, to the extent that the flame inside of me was nearly extinguished. So I'm now going to define myself like this:

Lollipops and Rainbows

Diary Entry: The Journey
Fictional, Informal

What we are looking for:

Narrated in first person	✓
Varied sentence structure	✓
High level vocabulary	✓
High level punctuation	✓
Correct grammar	✓
Maintaining informal tone and tense throughout	✓
Interesting and engaging	✓

Date 29th April 3017

"5, 4, 3, 2, 1 BLAST OFF!!!!"

Informal tone established with chatty voice, exclamations

And we were off! Up and away! This is the day that I had been waiting for… and now it arrived! My very first time in a space rocket. Obviously, some of my friends' parents had already been up in one – but now was my opportunity, as winner of a poetry competition. Yay!!!!

Use of the personal pronouns me/my/mine/us/we/our

The purpose of the trip was to find this new tiny planet and to decide how we were going to populate it. After our voyage of discovery, a huge committee meeting will be held with the wise elders, luminaries, leaders, teachers, healers and children to design how we would like the planet to be. But that's a story for another day.

153

Lollipops and Rainbows

High level vocabulary for description and imagery to engage the reader

Through the port holes I began to distinguish stars twinkling in the distant inky blackness; on the other side were the planets of my ancestors Andromeda and Pleiades, surrounded by a beautiful blue and green swirling star dust.

repetition for effect

We travelled on and on... further and further, until we reached the very edge of the Universe itself.

ellipsis - high level punctuation

opening sentences in different ways for variety

As the spaceship cruised along, its engines barely purring, we were able to hear the Universe's own song through special speakers.

varied sentence length and structure for interest

We could hear the planetary dance and the orchestral notes of galaxies, punctuated by melodic light from stars and moonbeams. We could hear deep melodies from Jupiter and Saturn drifting out to us in the furthest reaches of the Universe.

Clare Ford

Use of the rule of three for effect

It was the purest, deepest combination of sounds and vibrations I had ever heard. It was, simply, beautifully majestic.

If you would like tutoring support, book in your free exploration call with Clare and the SwitchedON! Team at:

https://switched-on.as.me/learn

and check out all the courses available to you at the SwitchedON! Academy

Educate * Empower * Elevate

Together, we are redefining education beyond academic success.

Printed in Great Britain
by Amazon